Roland Ward

The Sportsman's Handbook

to Practical Collecting, preserv ng, and artistic setting-up of trophies and

specimens to which is added a synoptical guide to the hunting grounds of

the world

Roland Ward

The Sportsman's Handbook
to Practical Collecting, preserving, and artistic setting-up of trophies and specimens
to which is added a synoptical guide to the hunting grounds of the world

ISBN/EAN: 9783337187071

Printed in Europe, USA, Canada, Australia, Japan

Cover: Foto ©Andreas Hilbeck / pixelio.de

More available books at **www.hansebooks.com**

THE SPORTSMAN'S HANDBOOK

TO

PRACTICAL COLLECTING,

PRESERVING,

AND

ARTISTIC SETTING-UP

OF

TROPHIES AND SPECIMENS.

TO WHICH IS ADDED

A Synoptical Guide to the Hunting Grounds of the World.

By ROWLAND WARD, F.Z.S.

London:

THE AUTHOR, 166, PICCADILLY.

SIMPKIN, MARSHALL, & CO., STATIONERS HALL COURT.

1880.

CHARLES DICKENS AND EVANS,
CRYSTAL PALACE PRESS.

𝕿𝖍𝖎𝖘 𝕭𝖔𝖔𝖐 𝖎𝖘 𝕯𝖊𝖉𝖎𝖈𝖆𝖙𝖊𝖉 𝖙𝖔

THE REVERED MEMORY OF

THE LATE HENRY WARD,

OF LONDON,

(MY FATHER),

WHOSE EMINENCE AS A PRACTICAL TAXIDERMIST,

AND AS

TRAVELLER, SPORTSMAN, AND NATURALIST,

I PRIZE LIKE AN INHERITANCE,

AND AFFECTIONATELY EMULATE.

ROWLAND WARD.

PREFACE.

I HAVE made an endeavour, by the following pages, to present for the sportsman-naturalist some information that may be valuable to him as derived solely from *experience*—either the accumulated experience of my family, of whom I am now the only representative in our profession, or the carefully collected experience of others in those parts of the subject where my own work has not carried me. My grandfather was a practical naturalist; my father, the late Henry Ward, became eminent in the same way, but with some remarkable advantages, having travelled much in pursuit of his profession in both hemispheres, and notably as the companion of Audubon, when that distinguished man was so greatly enriching and extending the field of natural history. My brother, Edwin Ward, late of 49, Wigmore Street, London, was one of the best known and most skilful operators in artistic taxidermy that we have ever had in this country. I have had the benefit of his advice and help, and have been greatly assisted, moreover, by the information given me by many travellers and true sportsmen. It has been my object to avoid mere speculative opinion, and to make the book as concise as might be.

It is only in comparatively recent times that taxidermy has been elevated to claim any real art position. What has been gained for it has not been achieved by mere skill, but by extended and more accurate observation of nature in its living forms—of the behaviour and habits of animals, not simply examination of their carcases, or what remained of those. Such observation, carefully and correctly recorded, is invaluable to the naturalist who seeks, by the preservation unimpaired of the natural features of an animal, to use the verisimilitude so obtained as an aid to art illustration. The material means for such a result are indeed important; but something more may be done with a prepared group of animals, or a single specimen, than preservation for the identification of details in anatomy or of outward appearance. Its value to the student may be preserved and increased by displaying its beauty truthfully to life, while the beauty is recognised for its own sake by even the unscientific. This is the cause I advocate, and the end I have in view.

R. W.

May 12th, 1880.

SPORTSMAN'S HANDBOOK.

INTRODUCTORY.

In starting from this or any other country on an expedition for collecting, that is likely or certain to separate him from the means and conveniences that he can command for money in settled and civilised communities, it is all important for the explorer or sportsman to provide himself carefully with everything he may want. But it is more important still that in doing so, he be able to define what his real wants are, and restrict the satisfaction of even these with skill to the smallest proportions. He should therefore quite judiciously consider what he really does need that it is desirable he should take with him, because he cannot obtain it so well elsewhere; but it is not well to imagine possible difficulties or wants, and endeavour to provide for them particularly. In regard to most of the apparatus, simplicity is to real usefulness like his skin is to a nigger. Attention should be paid to appropriateness of dress, but always with the recollec-

B

tion that in this respect a small modicum of native experience in any country is worth any amount of speculation out of it. That observation may also apply to most of the shifts and expedients of camp life. The well recorded experiences of good sportsmen, who have gone in similar fields before, are of infinite value to instruct; not for the simplicity of servile imitation in particulars, since the conditions may entirely differ, but as exemplifying the principles on which given means were applied to certain ends. Important factors in the consideration of these questions are the strength, stature, and constitution of the sportsman himself.

The progress of invention has of late years strengthened the position of the sportsman in respect of his armament, especially as regards great and dangerous game. He has wide choice of excellent weapons. In quite recent times this abundant facility has a little vexed the question, and some good sportsmen think they recognise the obtrusion of not indeed a fresh element, but more prominence for it—the endeavour to cloak deficiency of skill by increase of mere mechanical power in dealing with great game. In reality, the conditions have not changed for the true sportsman, who seeks rather an exercise of his skill and courage than the silly vanity of copious butchery. Indifferent ability may find compensation of a kind in that, but hardly the admiration of the judicious. In selecting particular weapons, each man will follow his bent; but on some points there is a consensus of opinion among good men that should strongly influence: That in the hands of a true sportsman of fine skill the chosen weapon for dangerous game should be light in relation to his personal strength, so that his ability to wield it easily may be without doubt : The "Express" rifle, on account of its easy carriage and manipulation, its power for internal wounding, its accuracy and extended point-blank range, is lauded by many as all-sufficient for ordinary game: For large game and dangerous animals a heavier bore is of course requisite, but one of not excessive capacity is considered sufficient for credit in good hands: The weapons should be carefully suitable to the stature of the sportsman, and to his length of reach, etc. There are some details, too, that have much to do with success—indeed, are almost, in such circumstances, a condition precedent of it—viz., the temper (hardness) of the ball, shot, or missile, the quality of the powder, and the quantum of the charge. These points should have careful attention. Experience on the field is the only true guide (our own or others'), and experiments are only valuable according to the conditions. Although sportsmen among great game have at all times had only such arms to deal with as they at the time possessed—sometimes arms that seem now quite primitive in comparison with modern weapons—the testing by sportsmen of such arms in real action is the only true test; indeed, eye and hand, as confident agents of undisturbed skilful judgment, are as important active forces for the result as the powder that utilises the best made missile, or the most accurate bore of any index. The gentleman who can, without erring, do all that is prescribed to clamped boards and puddled clay on an English sward, might find his calculations disturbed by the short rush of a rogue elephant, the sudden deadly spring of a tiger, or the oncoming of a heavy buffalo, who has at last become convinced that only one course is open to him.

The sooner the sportsman realises that his operations with great game cannot be reduced to the symmetry of a game of chess, the better will he be able to best guard his own safety and create success for himself on whatever field he may turn his attention to. In fact, nothing can be of more value to him in those circumstances than quick apprehensiveness, delicate tact, strong cool courage, and exquisite skill in the accurate use of his weapon. But underneath all this should lie a knowledge of what experience and investigation has taught us of how best to achieve our end; and one important phase of this knowledge is, how and where is it best to strike the game in a vital part, or in such way that the animal may be disabled. And here it must be remarked that no amount of book instruction will equal a small amount of experience; therefore it is well, when the game is killed and comes to be cut up, always to make a sufficient special investigation as to the course of your bullet in regard to its effect on the vital parts. In order to make clear what is the position of these points, some diagrams of animals representative of species are given, and on them the points are indicated. It may be said generally that the brain and the heart are the real organs to injure with vital effect; but to these must be added the spinal column. Now with different species of animals, in various circumstances, the conditions under which these parts can be reached vary considerably. We may consider the animals in two classes: (a) those that are dangerous, (b) those that are not seriously dangerous. These may again be divided into (c) animals that are in natural condition unsuspicious, or quiescent; (d) animals infuriate, aggressive, charging. To speak first of the

Felidæ. The place to hit a lion, if you are quite sure of your aim, as you may be if he is quiescent, is undoubtedly the brain. Now with tiger as well as lion, the brain is about the size of an apple, and small in comparison to the bony structure; the brain-pan is located about three or four inches to the rear of the eye (*vide* diagram). The heart is also indicated, and when the animal is broadside on, it can be pierced by a shot behind the shoulder. When he is charging

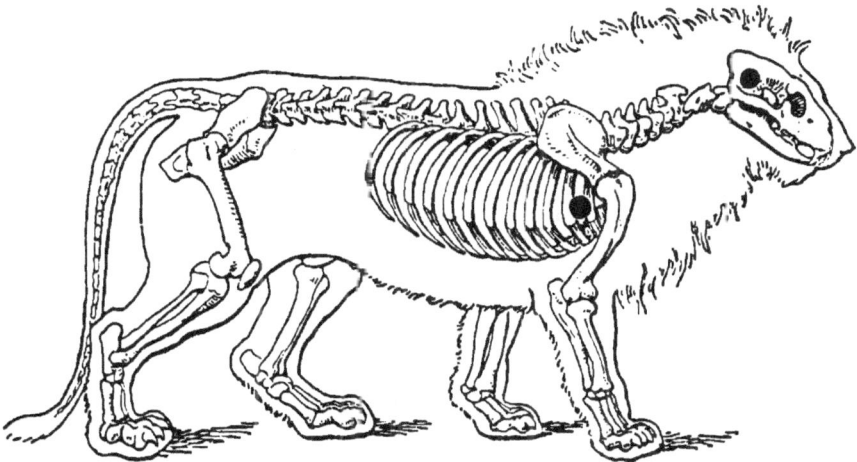

direct towards you, the best shot to deliver is a little to the right or left of the head, straight through the shoulder; by this you may perhaps pierce his heart, or possibly fracture the spinal cord; the bullet may traverse the body lengthwise with paralysing effect, or it will—which is most important—shatter the shoulder-bone and prevent his deadly spring. The rhinoceros is best killed by piercing the brain, or by fracture of the spinal cord. The brain is surely found in the region below the ear. The sportsman's position in regard to the animal will determine the possibility of his reaching the spinal cord. Tho hide of the Indian rhinoceros is harder than that of the African species, but on the living beast is easily permeable by hardened bullets; still, where there is room for choice, it is best to shoot between the folds.

In certain circumstances the charge of a Cape buffalo or a gaur is among the most dangerous experiences of the sportsman. The same general observations apply; but the neck and shoulder shot is to be

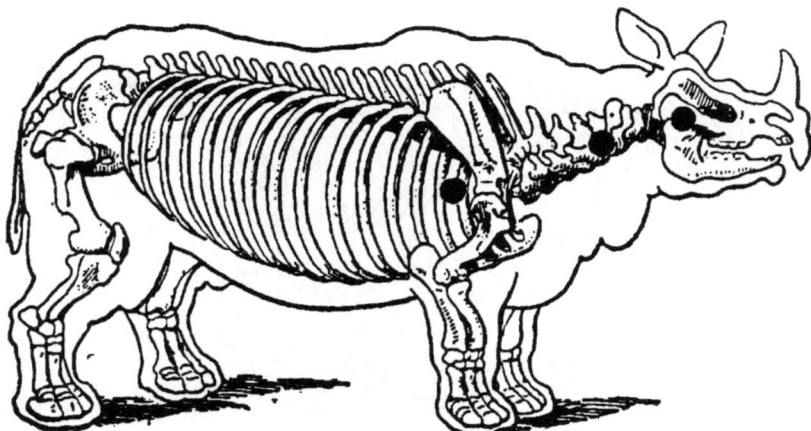

preferred. In regard to the elephant, there is a great difference between the African and the Indian. The skull of the first is convex in frontal form, while that of the Asiatic variety is concave. The brain is wonderfully small in comparison to the bony matter by which it is protected. The average weight of an elephant's brain is, say, nine pounds, which is but a fraction of the weight of the bone. The Asiatic elephant may be well shot dead while charging, if pierced in his forehead; but a similar shot would not be efficacious with the African. The brain of these creatures is

protected by a mass of cellular bone, which cannot
well be pierced by a bullet, unless it be directed
through the orifice of the ear. If he be charging
towards you, the best shot is in the chest. The
position of heart and brain is marked in the diagram.
When an African elephant is undisturbed, his great
ear will furnish a sure **direction for a deadly** shot.
Aim at the central portion of the outer edge.

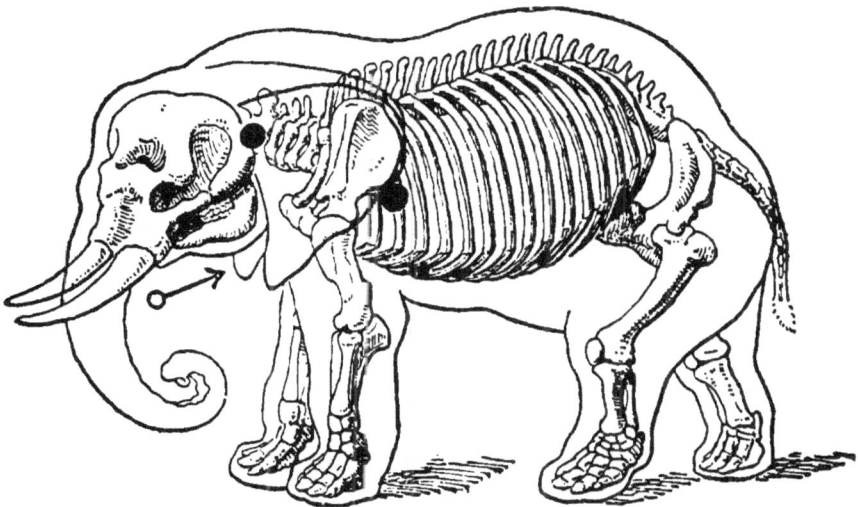

The hippopotamus if shot when he rises to the
surface of the water, should receive the bullet up his
nostril; that is the surest road to his brain. When
stricken the beast sinks, and it may be an hour or two
before his body rises; the time depends greatly on the
temperature of the water. If he is shot on the shore,
his heart should be aimed at behind the shoulder,
half-way up his body in the line of his leg—the
general rule. The seal should be shot in the brain,
but the locality of his brain is very deceiving. It is

peculiarly back toward the neck, as shown in the drawing.

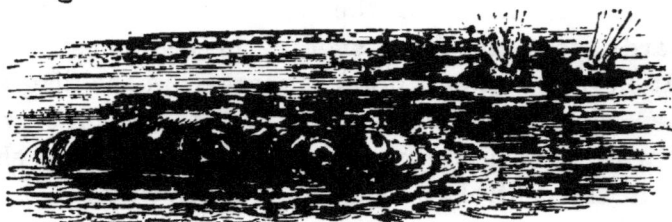

For collecting some small animals and birds, shot-guns of selected gauge, throwing appropriate shot, that need not be particularised here, are requisite.

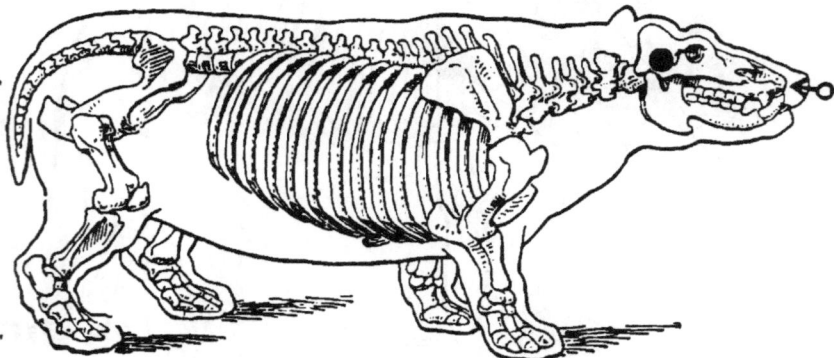

A more humble, but in its degree an equally useful implement for the collector, and one which he can employ to remarkable advantage, is the blow-pipe. Some savage races use this weapon—for it can be made by skill veritably a weapon—with as-tounding accuracy of aim and certainty of effect. In taking a lesson from them it is not necessary to misapply the means to any purpose for which the gun is more appropriate. But the collector will soon experience that, for many small specimens, he can use a blow-pipe with effect

where he may not be able to use firearms. The implement is so simple and so easily constructed that the
price of it is inappreciable. About three feet length
of any straight metal or wooden tubing, ¾-inch dia-
meter, through which a pellet the size of a marble
may be thrown, will serve well, but an even longer
tube may be chosen. The pellet should be of clay or
any putty, rolled in the hand to easily pass through
the barrel without too much windage. It should
not touch the mouth, but be lightly placed just in
the orifice, by stopping which with the thumb the
tube can be conveniently carried loaded, muzzle up,
ready for the most rapid use. To propel the pellet,
the puff must be sudden and powerful. There is
a proper way of effecting this. When a practitioner
first begins to use the blow-pipe, it is a common
error to eject the breath only direct from the lungs;
he should acquire the habit of inflating his cheeks,
so as to make a storage of wind, as it were, for each
shot; that, added to the breath from the lungs, gives
a force that will sometimes astonish him. The hand
follows the eye in aim, and practice will often develop
unthought-of proficiency. The particular uses of the
blow-pipe are these: that its operation is silent and
does not disturb, it is effective for small and mode-
rate-sized birds not on the wing, it is easily manipulated in a wood, it is easily obtainable anywhere, and
the ammunition costs nothing.

The question of traps, snares, etc., is one which
more concerns the collector or trader than the sportsman. Many specimens can of course be collected by
these means. A man's own taste will rule him in the
adoption of them better than any precept or instruction.
There are many ingenious devices used in America,
Scandinavia, and other fields for the capture of game

of all sizes, or the destruction of them rather. It will be found, however, that the ordinary gin, of whatever size it may be made, remains the really most efficacious of all such contrivances. The employment of dummies and decoys for birds, and especially for shore-birds, is interesting and useful. Probably in all parts of the world ingenuity can adapt this resource in degree. As a rule gregarious birds are those most subject to the fascination, for such it is. To give examples in our own country—wood-pigeons can be attracted thus : Any carpenter can make the shape of a wood-pigeon in rough; no legs need be shaped, but a stick should project from the lower part of the breast, so that the dummy can be fixed on the ground, or placed in a tree, as may be required; this figure must be painted in colour to represent the pigeon, and the paint must be " flatted," that is, not glossy. It is astonishing how the wild birds will come down to their haunts when they see this dummy there to assure them. In like manner plovers, gulls, and similar shore-birds may be decoyed. The decoy-duck is made buoyant to rest on the water, and is well known. Verisimilitude in regard to action is a great gain sometimes with these last-named, and is more important than mere details of feather. The following may be adduced as an instance of this : I once employed a decoy to deceive some sporting companions. They were looking for a shot in the evening twilight, and I provided one for them by hastily making a dab-chick of a bung, two wine-corks, and some wire. This rude image would float upright when ballasted with a stone at the end of a string; to this string I attached a live roach, and set the whole afloat under his guidance down the edge of some tempting reeds. The progress and occasional plunging

of the fish communicated the most natural action to
the dummy, and it received the complimentary recognition of many ounces of well-directed shot, until,
being well killed, the cork was secured, and *not* added
to the bag. This may afford a hint that can be
utilised by ingenuity where it seems to be a gain.

An useful part of the sportsman's kit is a photographic camera. This sounds alarming, as suggestive
of bulk and weight, and inconvenient dabbling with
scientific *minutiæ*, and perhaps dirty chemicals; but,
in truth, none of those fears need be realised. The
whole apparatus can be contained in a small case
eight inches each way. The tripod-stand—an important part—is made to fold into a stave two feet
long, about two inches thick. The sensitive plates are
dry and prepared ready for use before leaving home;
the inconvenience of properly using them, if there be
any inconvenience in developing the picture, is reduced
to a minimum, in no sense commensurate with the
gratification derived or the value of the work. An
animal may be photographed with its surroundings,
just as it fell; the picture may be made a nucleus of
interesting and most instructive memoranda, of obvious
value because such details are too often forgotten, or
the impression made by them effaced, just in proportion
as we move from the spot. Photographic pictures of
living *feræ naturæ*, in their native jungle or forest,
have indeed been thus taken, and hundreds of sea-
birds on the wing wheeling over an Indian headland,
have been reproduced with the most accurate representation of individual birds, so that when magnified
the picture presents the perfect specimen for our con-
templation—our more leisurely examination in fact—
than if we had witnessed them in their flight. These

are enormous advantages to gain if they be rightly estimated and used. The dry plates, in favourable circumstances, require only a second's exposure for a picture. They need not even be developed on the spot, if inconvenient; the undeveloped negative will keep good for months. The most portable plates are those four inches by three inches; they are sufficiently large for most useful purposes, though of course larger plates for larger pictures can be carried. It is all important that the camera and apparatus should be good, the tripod true and firm.

The knives or other implements should be as few and simple as is consistent with meeting the real need efficiently; a tiger can be perfectly skinned by a skilful hand with a shoemaker's knife, price threepence-halfpenny. It is highly important that some preparation should be made for efficient and accurate record of scientific data, concerning natural features that are [evanescent, such as colour of the eye, of a bird's bill and legs, etc.; but it is not too much to say that the whole of such apparatus may, by well considered ingenuity, be carried in the compass of a case whose capacity is measured in a few inches. It must be borne in mind before all things, that the value of any object secured and preserved depends on the completeness with which all its natural features are saved, as well as the condition in which they are kept. This is true in degree for whatever purpose the object be designed, but it is essential in regard to specimens for the illustration of natural history.

GENERAL OBSERVATIONS FOR THE COLLECTOR.

DIRECTLY a specimen is secured inspect the eye, and make a concise memorandum of its colour and any peculiarity of its appearance. A similar note should be taken of any colour on the bills, legs, etc., of birds (the brilliancy of which may fade), and particular note should be preserved of eyelids, the colour of them, if they have colour; and the same may be said of wattles and all such features of naked skin, because most frequently when these parts dry, the colours not only fade, but change sometimes absolutely; and the taxidermist at home may be led to a wrong conclusion. Never omit, and never defer the making of these memoranda, or instant decision on the necessity for it.

It is better that specimens of all warm-blooded creatures should be cold before they are operated on.

In dealing with birds care should be taken, directly they are shot, that the plumage be not broken, or injured by putting many of them together in a bag; and that the blood from one fresh specimen does not injure another. Instantly plug up with cotton wool the throat, nostrils, and all shot holes. Rare examples can be isolated in a cone of paper, or otherwise, as soon as they are secured. It is often a scientific gain to save at least the *sternum* or breastbone, with the *caracoids*, the *furcula* (merry-thought), and *scapula* of birds, and the skull when the skin is not saved.

Pay particular and unvarying attention to the ticketing of specimens.

Tickets of convenient, durable material should be provided. Note thereon:—Date; a number; where killed; native name; scientific names; sex; habitat; habits observed, as to the eye, etc.; and peculiarities

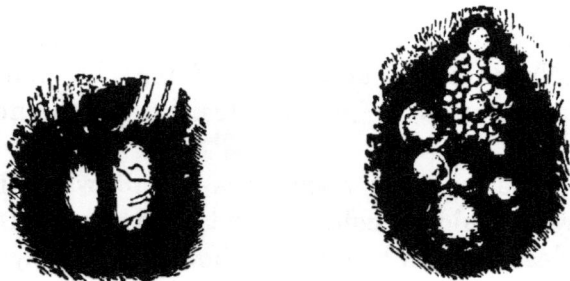

of colour. Any other peculiarities, or facts noticed. To sex a bird, examine the inner regions of the loins, and if male mark it ♂, and if female thus ♀.

This question of ticketing, and the preparation of the ticket is all important. There is little, if any doubt, that the brilliant colours on a fresh, healthy specimen, at the moment it falls, are always deteriorated, sometimes altered, under treatment by any preservative. Therefore, when the "colours" are noted, if possible, the collector should always put on his ticket a blot of water-colour pigment as near as may be, to reproduce the brightness and quality of the tint. This may need some ingenuity, but will be found not

difficult; a few cakes of water-colour and a brush take
little space; the gain by this record will be great.
The sexing is of much consequence; to determine it,
where necessary, involves a slight dissection, when
the appearances will be found as on page 14.

Corresponding tickets to those on the skins, etc.,
should be attached firmly to skulls, horns, bones, etc.,
and saved so that exact identification may be easy and
certain.

Be as forethoughtful as possible in all operations;
and be careful that no blood or grease, or juices from
the offal, injure the feathers or fur.

It is generally far better to attend to the preserving
of your own specimens, than to trust to native agents
or servants; if you are compelled to trust to them
at all, never sanction the use of lime in the materials
they employ, even as a small constituent. Some natural
substances (berries, etc.), used by natives, will change
colour on specimens; the yellow ground of a leopard
skin may be thus changed to reddish brown, etc.

PROCESSES OF PRESERVATION.

In regard to the preservation for after treatment of the skins of great game, it would be easy here to quote many recipes of approved efficiency, and, in given circumstances, not open to doubt. But, for the particular conditions of the explorer, the *simplest* process that is safe and good is the *best*. I think that the materials carried may be reduced to two, viz. a quantity of dry powdered alum and a supply of spirits of turpentine. How these should be applied I shall presently explain.

For the treatment of bird-skins a supply of arsenical soap should be carried. It can be compounded of the following ingredients :

Camphor	5 ozs.
White Arsenic, in powder ...	2 lbs.
Yellow Soap	2 lbs.
Lime, in powder	4 ozs.

Melt the soap completely by heat in a small quantity of water, and add the lime; then remove it from the fire and stir in the arsenic; next add the camphor, previously rubbed to powder with a little spirits of wine, and mix the whole thoroughly, till it has the consistence of paste. Preserve it in carefully closed glazed vessels, labelled "Poison." To use it, mix the quantity required with cold water to the consistence of clear soup, and apply it with a brush to the inside of the skins.

There are two methods of preserving animals, or the skins of animals, on the spot where they are collected till they can be transmitted for definite treatment by skilled practitioners at home : viz. (1) by means of preservative applications, so that natural decay and the ravages of insects, etc., may be prevented; (2) by immersion and packing of specimens, on proper principles, in spirit, or in pickle. Convenience and obvious desirability will rule the adoption of either plan, and the application of it to particular specimens. Animals taken whole can be dissected; and examples of absolutely new species, or specimens of rare occurrence, may, at discretion, be transmitted thus with many advantages. Generally pickle, or brine, preserves natural colours of specimens better than spirit.

PRESERVATIVES ON THE FIELD.—The skins of all mammalia, of fish, and of reptiles can be efficiently preserved for transmission home, by the simple dry alum process; but the skins of birds should be treated with arsenical soap. These resources, simple as they are, will be found sufficient, and they have this distinct advantage, that in the ultimate treatment of the specimen for permanent keeping, there are fewer difficulties to be surmounted by the skilled naturalist or the curer of skins. When salt, for instance, is used, or the lime of native Indian dressers (the most destructive in the world), or the vegetable curing of the Australian skins, there is often more trouble to take *out* of the pelt the deleterious substance, so that the process of decay may be stopped, than the specimen is worth. The skins of birds must not be treated with alum, or they become fatally brittle; the arsenical soap has a contrary effect, and softens the skin. All specimens or examples of either genus must be protected from the ravages of insects; and to do this the simplest means is the copious and judicious application of spirit of turpentine; but this must not be applied to birds, because it dissolves the grease that is more or less found in every bird-skin, and thus the metallic colours of plumage become permanently robbed of their brilliancy, and birds of white plumage

c

are soiled by a yellowish stain. Where, however, there are no metallic colours to be preserved, the advantage of turpentine as a preservative may be gained, if it be applied lightly and with skill to the surface of the feathers, and not poured over the skin, as we might do with the skin of a mammal. The best way is to apply it with a saturated pad of cotton wool.

THE ALUM PROCESS.—The material to be employed is powdered burnt alum. When the skin of a mammal has been removed, the very first thing to do, without loss of time, is to "flesh it," which means to carefully clean the pelt of all superfluous flesh or fat. This having been done, spread the skin hair downwards and peg it out flat, unless you have a frame or other better mechanical means of stretching it. Of course of small animals in some portions of which the bone is retained—for instance the leg — the skin must not be pegged out; and indeed where means exist of avoiding it, do not "peg out" at all, as the skin is always somewhat injured by that process, and sometimes is irreparably torn, therefore avoid such injuries if you can. The fact of drying induces shrinkage; so arrange your skin that as it shrinks it cannot wrinkle into folds, for in those, if anywhere, the ravages of insects will lie. In cold climates, perhaps, pegging and stretching may be avoided altogether. The skin having been spread out flat with the pelt uppermost, proceed to rub in the alum. This should be done with the hand carefully to cover every portion, and the supply of alum should not be stinted. It must be particularly applied to the lips, ears, feet, and other fleshy parts that have been prepared in skinning to receive the preservative (see p. 30). The whole pelt having been treated thus by hand, sprinkle it with the alum till it is regularly and well covered. The skin should be left thus until it is dry, and it will be found that the astringent alum will dry it with rapidity. But during this time it is most necessary to watch it well, so that if there appear a tendency in any part of it to "taint," which would cause the hair to "slip" or come off, the preservative may be instantly applied on the hair side as well as the pelt wherever requisite. When the skin is dry it must be conveniently folded, hair side inwards, for packing, that is if it be of large game and requires folding. First turn the hair side up and pour turpentine freely over it till the skin is thoroughly anointed. Note that with long-haired animals the turpentine reach the roots of the hair; sprinkle the pelt side; but it is not necessary to anoint that so fully as the fur. It is well, when convenient, to put some dry material in

the folds to prevent contact between the inside of the skin and the fur; and, as occasion may serve, the skin should be unfolded and inspected, and more turpentine or preservative applied to parts if necessary. In the process just described the astringent alum is applied to preserve the skin, and the turpentine to protect it against insects. The ravages of these pests in a hot climate, such as India, are indescribably vexatious, and must be carefully guarded against. The principal of all the marauders is a beetle about a quarter of an inch long, of a dark dirty colour with a transverse band of dull yellow; he does not often fly, being generally more busily engaged on carefully collected skins; but he can fly. His common name and his scientific name are "The Bacon Beetle;" or *Dermestes Ladratus*; but as

he is so veritable an enemy it is best not to rely on his
cognomen, but on instant recognition for immediate ex-
termination, therefore his portrait life-size is given on
page 19. Now this insect does not like any spirit; but
the one spirit he really dreads as fatal to his constitution is turpentine. In the colder climates benzine and
similar spirits are sometimes used and with efficacy, but
these evaporate more rapidly in warmer temperature,
and turpentine, if only because of its less rapid evaporation, is at all times to be preferred. I have sometimes
unpacked trophies to discover the hair entirely removed
from the pelt by the exertions of the *Dermestes*; and in
like manner I have received skulls in London that have
been imperfectly cleaned of flesh, from which I have
shaken hundreds upon hundreds of fattened lively
specimens. I gave them the turpentine they should
have had in India. Sometimes they will recover
activity after the milder influence of benzine. The
alum process is quite sufficient for *Pachydermata*.

PICKLE.—Another process that is frequently most
convenient on shipboard, or, according to the conditions, is that of "pickling." The skin having been
removed from the carcase and cleaned, instead of being
laid out for drying, should be thickly covered over the
flesh side with powdered alum, the lips, eyelids, feet,
etc., being particularly treated; then it should be
folded in a convenient form, and thus be immersed
in a barrel of brine, or what is technically called
"liquor"—in fact, parts of alum and salt dissolved
in water, in the proportion of 6 lbs. of alum and
3 lbs. of salt, sea salt if possible. Dissolve both in
a small quantity of hot water sufficient to make a
gallon, and let the liquid cool before the specimen is
immersed. The skin must be sweet and fresh at the

time of placing it in pickle, or the operation will not succeed. The vessel must be kept closed. A number of skins may be placed in the same barrel, which is then ready, when quite filled, and closed, for storing, or for transit. If thought more convenient to make the package lighter for travelling, the skins can, when they have been thoroughly pickled for a few days, be taken out, spread open and dried, then repacked. This, however, is an operation requiring obviously great judgment, as if it be imperfectly carried out the consequence may be ruinous.

A conspicuous exemplification of the advantages in this process of brine-pickling, was afforded by the great elephant trophy brought from South Africa by H. R. H. the Duke of Edinburgh. In this case the system was adopted in manner following : The entire skin of the mighty beast was preserved. The animal was undoubtedly one of the largest examples ever brought to this country of the African species. His height at the withers was 10 ft. ; from tip of trunk to tip of tail, 23 ft. 5 in. ; girth, 16 ft. 6 in. ; from top of head to end of trunk, 11 ft. 3 in. ; circumference of head, 10 ft. ; from ear to ear, 9 ft. ; length of ear, 4 ft. 6 in. The skull and tusks weighed more than 3 cwt. ; the skin of the head when taken from pickle, weighed 3 cwt. 6 lbs. The weight of the whole skin when taken from pickle, was 20 cwt. 7 lbs. The weight of the entire elephant in the flesh was 4 tons 8 cwt. 4 lbs. On the field the skin, having been duly prepared, was folded in this wise : the flanks with skin of legs and feet were folded inwards, each half-way, so that the inner surfaces or flesh side were outwards ; then the skin of the head was in like manner turned back, the trunk being disposed of longitudinally down the centre between the edges of the flanks ; and the tail end with nether extremities was similarly folded back to meet the trunk. The whole skin was then rolled as tightly as possible round the head, and carefully tied at both ends of the bale. In this condition it was placed in a great barrel which was then completely filled with

liquor, and properly coopered for transmission to this country. On arrival in London, when the head of the barrel was removed, the perfect success of this mode of transport was at once apparent. There was no unpleasant odour. On taking out the mass and unfolding the skin, it was noticeable that every part of the surfaces had been properly acted on, and there was not a single tainted fold. At that time it had been upwards of a year in the barrel. The old pickle was removed, the skin was refolded and restored to the barrel with a supply of fresh liquor, and the cask was re-coopered. In this manner the skin was preserved for upwards of three years more, until the decision as to how this great trophy should be treated was arrived at. The magnificent head was mounted, and is now in Clarence House; the feet (which supply an index of his size) were utilised for ornamental purposes, while the hide was cut up and converted to use; a considerable portion being made into walking sticks, that formed appropriate mementoes.

The skulls of large mammalia are always removed from the skins. It is important for the proper preservation of the skulls of *Felidæ*, that they should be protected from injury to, or loss of, the teeth. This is best done as follows : When the skull has been boiled (not too much or it loosens the sutures) or soaked, and properly cleaned, and the teeth painted with wash about half-an-inch thick, it should be tied up in a calico bag and placed in a separate compartment of the packing-case designed for it. Stuffing should moreover be put into each compartment to prevent the specimen from being shaken, and so injured. The wash for teeth mentioned above can be well made of wax; as the tooth dries it often splits up, the bony structure as well as the enamel; wax tends to prevent this action.

It should be mentioned in case of need, that many strong mineral and vegetable astringents can be used with more or less success besides arsenic, alum, and salt; such as saltpetre, powdered green vitriol, or sulphate of iron, corrosive sublimate, etc. It is also maintained that white arsenic applied in dry powder, or mixed with spirits of wine to the consistency of treacle, and put on with a brush, is the best preservative of all. Of vegetable substances, gum kino, oak bark, willow bark, catechu, powdered nutgalls, or any such material rich in tannin, are available; and strong spices or strong tobacco powdered will keep off insects. A large skin, in default of anything better, may be plentifully dressed on the inside with wood ashes. The virtue of wood ashes really consists in their detergent properties; for, containing as they do a large proportion of potash, the fat is thereby converted into soap, and sometimes in this condition is immediately brought away by the hand, or the scraper, and as a preservative, excepting under difficult conditions, the effect is cleanly and good. Remember that there is a difference in ashes, depending on the wood employed. Oak is one of the best.

Fish.—The proper preservation of fish is undoubtedly a matter of some difficulty. Naturalists are perhaps not generally aware of how few examples of foreign fish reach this country in a condition that admits of effective after treatment, or how special a branch of the art it is to set them up effectively and well. The ordinary processes are : (1) to plunge and bottle them in spirits ; and we all know the effect of that on the evanescent colouring, as well as on the natural contour of the specimens ; (2) when they are skinned (see p. 46), to apply alum to those parts where the flesh cannot be perfectly removed, so that it may be dried, and to apply arsenical soap on the inside, for preservation of the skin.

Reptiles.—The skins of crocodiles, alligators, and

the larger reptiles having been removed (see p. 46), must be manipulated as follows : Clean them of all flesh as perfectly as you can; this, however, cannot be done very completely about the head, or the feet of a large example, and to those parts alum must be applied in plenty to dry up the flesh as well as may be. The roof of the mouth can be cleaned, and the tongue must come away. With smaller specimens that can be skinned over the skull to the lips, a similar application must be made where it seems necessary. To the inner part of the skins some arsenical soap, or wood ashes may be put; but, really, the preservatives are not nearly so necessary as in the case of warm-blooded mammals. Indeed turpentine that will protect them from insects will afford nearly all the protection they need. The skin can be rolled or folded for transmission. With snakes, the skin dried flat can be rolled from the tail like a ribbon, the belly side inwards on account of the scales. Small specimens of any species will go in spirits. Carbolic is a useful agent in cleansing all reptiles.

IMMERSION IN SPIRIT.—Something must be specially said about this mode of preservation, for there is absolute necessity that it should be properly carried out, or nearly all the advantage of the resource is neutralised. Either fish or reptiles, or even birds, that may be sent home in spirits, should be treated in this way : First provide a tub, or other convenient vessel, full of the spirit, wherein the specimens can be put as a preliminary measure, so that the mucus, water, etc., may be drawn out of them. Before placing them in this a moderate incision should be made, with as little disturbance as possible, in the belly, so that the spirit may permeate all parts. Keep the specimens

in this spirit from a week to ten days, then transfer
them to fresh spirit, and let them remain in that for
about two weeks more, before finally you remove
them to the vessel or vessels of spirit in which they
are to be packed for the remainder of the journey.
Reptiles, being less watery than fish, generally require
only one change.   The first tub of spirit may be used
for more than one set of animals, but will of course
decrease in strength by the addition of the water
drawn from them ; the second spirit should be
stronger ; the third quite strong enough to be readily
inflammable.   They will then be safe for more than
six months, and can be sent home.   Proof spirit,
diluted about one-half with water, is perhaps the best
to use, but rum or gin serves well.   The specimens
can be packed for transmission in great numbers thus:
Wrap each fish or reptile in a piece of linen or cotton
rag, and arrange them to rest closely in an appropriate
vessel that can be then filled completely with spirit.
A wooden packing-case, well lined with tin, that can
be hermetically soldered up when quite full of the liquid,
serves well.   Of insects, beetles can be transmitted
in spirit.

INSECTS.—The majority of insects having been properly stored as directed (see p. 48), require little more
than a supply of camphor, or cyanide of potassium, to
protect them from decay.   Mites sometimes appear in
them as an evidence of taint, and then the best means
for destroying the intruders is benzine.   But some very
large moths, butterflies, and beetles require a different
treatment.   In such cases the body must be opened by
a longitudinal section on that side not intended to
be displayed, and as much matter must be removed as
can be got away without impairing the specimen.

The cavity thus created should be filled with corrosive sublimate in a dry powdered condition, and the incision must be neatly and skilfully closed over it.

SKINNING AND PREPARATION.

THE apparatus necessary for the skinning of animals is really very simple, and I strongly advise that it

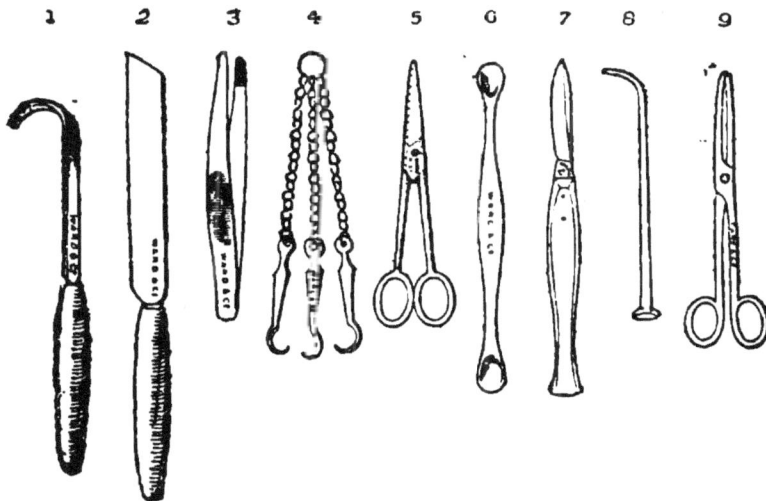

1   2   3   4   5   6   7   8   9

should be kept to the simplest proportions. It is the skill with which the knife is wielded that is more important than the best of knives. A shoemaker's knife, a small saw, a pair of pliers, and perhaps a pair of cutting pincers, are all that are required for operating on the most important game. Some small implements for small specimens being added, this is all the kit that need be carried. To understand the principle of the thing, and to adapt that principle in practice with ingenuity and judgment to the particular conditions that present themselves, is the true learning; and to

cumber the mind with numberless minute memoranda
of other travellers' experiences in emergencies that
may never be our lot, is an useless task. Enrich the
recollection with all that experience brings to bear on
the subject in deductions, to illustrate or to inform,
but not to copy simply of necessity. The best
operator is he who does what is right to carry out his
purpose, carefully, on true principles, according to the
means at his command, and the advantages of surrounding conditions; he who simply copies what others
have done in given circumstances, forgets, probably,
the conditions under which they succeeded, and that
the conditions are not necessarily the same in his case.
Let a man be master of the occasion and his position
will be good, even if it is different from any that has
gone before. Now what has to be done is simply
this, and the remark applies equally to large or small
game, mammalia, birds, reptiles, or fishes. A beast
having been slain, or a specimen secured, we have to
remove the skin, preserving the exterior natural
features, as completely as possible; then the skin—cut
as little as may be—because it would otherwise decom-
pose under the influence of climate, etc., such decay
must be averted by the application of preservatives,
and when it is packed so that it is protected, the
trophy may be sent home. But the preservative and
precautions necessary in an Indian or African climate,
may be modified in North America, and in highlands
or lowlands, in forests or exposed positions. There is,
in fact, no preservative, or book recipe, or tale of other
persons' experience, that can compare in value to
quick true judgment, and cultivated common sense.
I shall describe in as much detail as appears necessary
the skinning and preparation of one animal represen-

tative of each class; and my reader must trust himself
to adapt the practice by the light of his own judgment
to the specimens, large or small, with which he may
have to deal; and he will soon find his practice surpass
in usefulness the most compendious (and cumbersome)
book of recipes and directions.

LARGE GAME.—When the great game is secured,
and is ready for the operation, first turn the animal on
its back, and, stretching apart the fore and hind legs,
proceed to remove the skin. In all cases where the
skin is wanted entire, this is best done by making an
incision from the corner of the mouth, through the
medial line of the belly to the extremity of the tail;
but in doing this cut only just through the skin, and
be careful not unnecessarily to injure the carcase, or
especially the intestines; next make lateral incisions
in order to strip the limbs; for the forelegs from the
edge of the central incision through the armpit, along
the inner side of the limbs, the line of incision inclin-
ing slightly to the outer portion, in order that the
seam may be less perceptible when the perfect specimen
is mounted. A like process through the groin is
necessary for the hind legs. These incisions thus
made leave the skin in form of tongue-pieces over the
breast. First apply the knife to these points, and
detach the skin round to the spine and along the tail.
In doing so it is necessary to clear the limbs, and great
care must be taken to leave intact the natural features
of the foot. The last metacarpal and metatarsal bones
may be left in the skin, whether with the smaller
specimens of *Felidæ* or *Cervidæ*; but in the big animals
it is better to remove them altogether. Now turn over
the carcase, and draw back the whole skin over the
head, exercising particular care in separating the ears

and the eyes from the skull. Similar care must be taken as to the lips, for if the rim of the eyelids be severed by the scalpel the injury spreads in a remarkable manner, often so badly as to render the damage seriously conspicuous. The ears should be parted from the skull close to the bone, or the lower structure of them will present too large an aperture. The lips must be cut off close to the gums. Having thus taken off the skin, it must be cleared of all superfluous fat and flesh—and all the fat and flesh is superfluous. The cartilaginous portion of the ear must be turned through. The lip must be treated thus: Pass the knife betweeen the mucous lining and the outer skin all round the mouth, so as to admit of the preservative penetrating this thick portion of the specimen completely. The eyelids and the feet must each be treated in a similar manner for the same reason. Be careful that the claws or hoofs are well kept.

A fruitful source of trouble to the sportsman in Ceylon, India, Africa, etc., is the proper treatment of an Elephant's foot. This feature is a recognised trophy, as well as the head, because it is a gauge of the size of the specimen, and because in ordinary circumstances the skin of this mighty beast is so difficult of transport, and although it can be converted by skill into innumerable articles of domestic utility, the value of it in private hands is not always appreciated. It is different with the foot, excepting that it is particularly adaptable for conversion into useful articles, without impairing its natural history significance. The foot should be severed at least eighteen inches from the ground—that is to say, the skin should be severed. Cut the skin down the back of the foot right across the sole to the toe; a second cut must be made across the sole so as to form a cross with the first, but these incisions must not be carried so far that they would be visible when the foot is imposed on the ground. Now separate the skin from the flesh, and bring the casing of the foot away in one piece. Clean it carefully, and apply powdered alum both inside and outside, then place it to dry in the shade, taking good care that the skin does not fold, and is in all parts accessible to the air. It is not absolutely necessary that the skin dry in natural shape, but it is important that the foot be protected from insects, and to this end, when the specimen is quite dry, saturate it as far as possible with turpentine. Rhinoceros and Hippopotamus can be treated in the same way.

Something must be specially said as to the head. It frequently happens that it is desired to save the head for preservation as a trophy, while the other part of the skin is either abandoned or saved for a rug. Heads with antlers or horns are prepared for preservation either in the naked bone or to be set up to imitate living nature. For this last, care must be exercised to take the skin of the whole neck. Make the incision up the back of the neck, over the head between the ears until the horns are reached; if they are wide apart cut between them right and left, carrying the incision right round the burr of each horn. In separating the skin from the burr the knife should be used neatly with a plunging action of the point, so that not a particle of hair or skin be sacrificed at this part. He is a bad workman who leaves a morsel of the skin attached to the bone. In clearing the scalp be very careful not to let the knife injure the skin; the knife must be deftly used. But there are other features with which this skill is more important still—to wit,.

the eyes, the nostrils, and the ears. The delicate skin round the eye is nearly hairless ; it must not on any account be torn or jagged. In a head the eyes and the nose are the most prominent parts, first claiming notice. In treating the nostrils and upper lip operate from inside the mouth ; sever the lip neatly high up the gum, over the teeth; and in like manner detach the lip below. The skin will present in these portions a particular thickness, into which, from the inside, a neat midway incision must be carried all along, so that the preservative may penetrate and be carefully rubbed into the cut to the end that these parts may be saved properly. The alum process is best; but if more convenient the skins may be preserved in pickle (see p. 20). Clean the skin well of all fat and flesh ; rub in the alum, but not on the outside of the nose, and hang up the skin to dry. If there should appear any likelihood of the short hair round the eyes and nostrils slipping, apply some alum judiciously there. Be sure to save the lower jaw. When the head is of Wapiti, and is to be set up thus, it may be a matter of great convenience to pack the horns, and to do that the skull, to which they are attached, may be sawn in two, longitudinally, by which much space may be gained. But if the trophy is to be mounted in the naked bone, this severance is quite inadmissible, and it should in no case be adopted with smaller heads, which are, in fact, almost destroyed by it, the skull is thereby weakened, and at the end of the journey broken to pieces. Such a state of things necessitates great extra labour and expense even if the injury can ever be repaired. Some North American trophies recently received have come in a deplorable condition from this sort of injury, by which neither convenience nor economy can have been secured. For preservation in the bone, the flesh may be roughly taken off, and the skull be cleaned by boiling, by maceration in a stream, or by burying it for a proper time in an ant-hill. But be sure and keep the specimen from dogs or other animals. In regard to the ears, when the skin is off, and you have separated the cartilage close to the bone, trim it neatly with the scissors of all that is not wanted inside, but do not take too much, or an unsightly hole may appear when the head comes to be mounted. Next insert the thumb and finger from the inside so as to separate the inner from the outer skin, forming, as it were, a flat bag; do not carry this separation too near the edges. Into the division preservative must be carefully put. It is my practice to fill the space with composition, which keeps the ear for ever the proper size and shape. The old way of sewing a piece of card on the outside is not good, it allows the skin to shrivel and shrink, and its natural beauty is seldom or never to be restored. Some horns (as *Ovis Ammon*) have "bearers," or a bony core, from which the horns may be detached and packed separately; in this instance the skull should be kept, and so much of the bearers as seems superfluous may be removed.

SMALL MAMMALIA.—These can be preserved for dissection and preparation, when necessary, in spirit; or, as described in the cases of large skins, in liquor. When they are treated thus, incision must be carefully made in the trunk, and the intestines, with as much blood, mucus, etc., as possible removed; the liquid will then penetrate, and the carcase should be soaked in spirit or liquor for some time, in order that the juices of the body may be drawn out into it, and then the specimen should be removed into fresh spirit, strong enough to light with a match, and so packed. The receptacle should be quite full.

In preparing the skin the following course should be adopted: the skull and the bones of the legs are to be left in the skins. The animal being placed on its back, make incision from the *sternum* (breast-bone) to the root of the tail, next separate the skin from the carcase, so far as can be conveniently reached, and sever the limbs from the body at the shoulders and thighs. Each limb can then be drawn out—as a glove might be turned inside out—but the bone must not be separated at its junction with the toe, or the skin of the foot or leg be in any way injured. Now remove the muscles from the bone. This can best be done by cutting the tendons near the toes, and carefully drawing the whole mass away at one operation. It must come in one piece, not piecemeal. The bone will now be clean. Clean the skin of the limb, and at the same time the other parts of the skin of all superfluous flesh and fatty matter. Dress the inside with arsenical soap, and apply freely powdered alum all over it, but particularly to the fleshy parts, as the eyes, nose, lips, feet, etc. Then replace the bones in the limbs, having previously, if possible, bound them with tow, or similar material, so as to replace the muscle that has been removed. Place a portion of stuffing in the skin of the head and trunk, and suspend the specimen to dry.

The tail must be treated in this way: sever the *vertebræ* from the trunk close up to the body, leaving the tail in its sheath. Turn back the skin until enough of the tail protrudes to fasten securely with a string, that can be attached to a hook, or tree, or other firm holding. Then with a cleft stick, or the handle of your pliers, pull the skin sheath down toward the tip, and the *vertebræ* will come away whole, wrinkling the skin to the end. Shake powdered alum into the cavity, or, if preferred, insert arsenical paste on a stick.

SKELETONS.—When it is desired to save the skeleton of an animal, the procedure should be this: Having removed the skin, cut the fleshy parts away; this need not be done too closely, neither is it necessary nor desirable in the operation to separate the joints. The bony frame, or its portions, should next be placed where they can be covered by water, the object being first to extract all blood, therefore it is well, as occasion requires, to pour off and renew the water, until it comes away comparatively clear. The next operation is to leave the skeleton in the liquid till the soft portions putrefy, and so leave the bone clean. The large bones that contain marrow must be perforated at either end, where the holes will be least observed, and returned to the water. They will come clean in due course like the others. The complete operation of this putrefying will occupy several months, but is expedited by a warm temperature. When the decay of the fleshy matter is complete, the bones must be cleaned by hand, and should then be immersed for a few (say 6) hours in a weak solution of lime-water. The bones are by this time quite separated, and it is all-important to care that not one, even the smallest, be missing; the loss of one little portion vitiates the usefulness of all—a skeleton incomplete in any part is of no value. The bones must next be bleached by the simple action of the atmosphere in the shade. If the operator be abroad the bones may then be packed for transmission; if he be where skilled assistance can be obtained, they are fit for articulation.

BIRDS.—Having seen that the cotton plugging of the throat, nostrils, and the shot-holes is safe, the first operation is to break the wing-bones (*humeri*) close to the body. If the bird be a large specimen, the most convenient and effectual way to do this is to hold the bird pendent by his wing against the edge of a table or board, so that the bone may be fractured by the sharp blow of a stick, with as little rough treatment as may be. But the doing this skilfully is indeed the gist of the whole work; there is a proper way of doing it. The wing must be held by the upper feathers, pressed flat by all the fingers against the palm, so that the manipulation do not crush, or even seriously disturb the lay of the fibre. The blow with the stick must be a firm quick stroke of sufficient strength to complete the fracture, not simply to bruise the flesh, or so rough as in breaking the bone to unduly mangle it. The firmness of the board or table-edge is a great element in the neatness of this operation. The action of the hand will best be seen on the accompanying illustration.

This is the method for treating large birds. In the case of small specimens—that is anything less in size than a blackbird—the same bone may be well broken by the thumb and finger, or at most by the forceps. The wing-bone being thus broken, place the bird on his back, the head toward you, in order that your knife may, what is technically called, "go with the grain of the feather." By this I mean that the point of the knife should be deftly inserted under the skin just at the end of the breast-bone; raise the skin

till it bags, then press the knife forward in one clean
continuous incision down to the vent, so that the skin

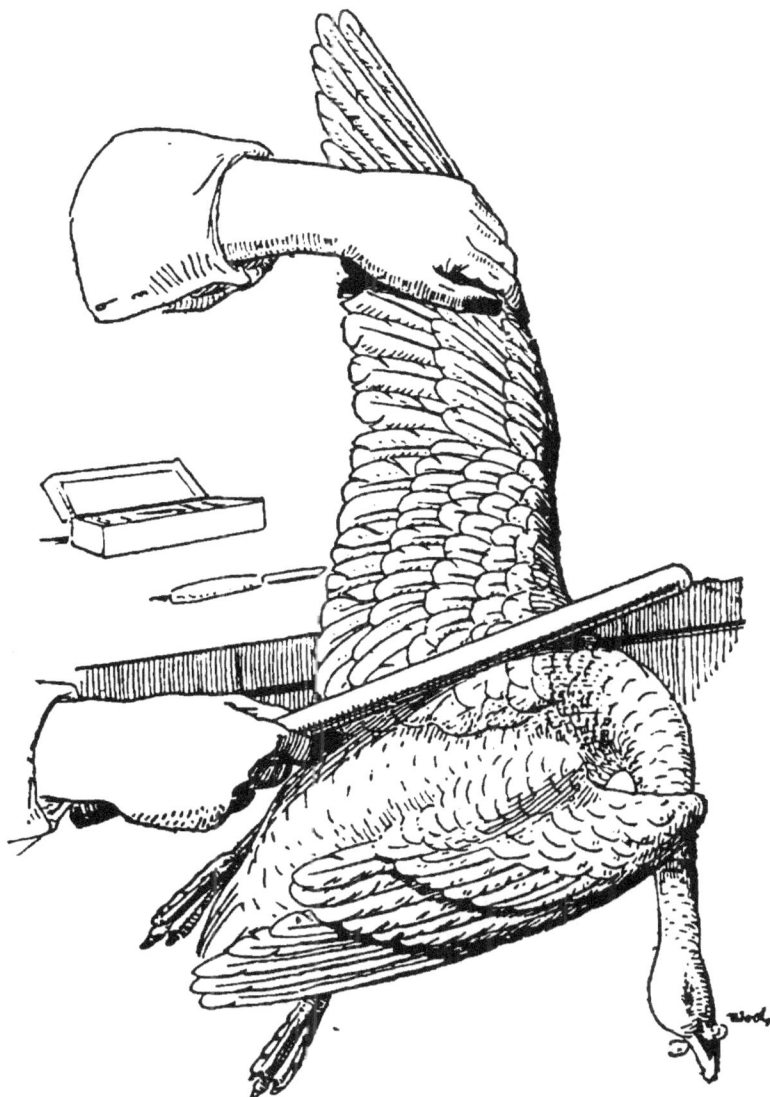

be separately severed, but the flesh remain uninjured.
Amateurs are constantly inclined to make their first
incision from too high or too low a point; and the

mistake of injuring the stomach in any part is another
danger that besets them.   The opening thus made in
the skin should be no larger than is necessary for the
withdrawal of the body.   For this purpose only is it
made.   Indeed with birds that have breasts of

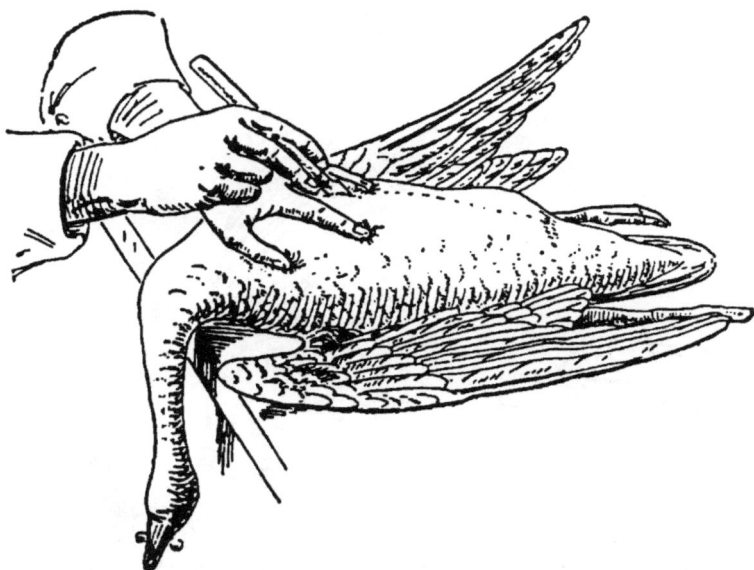

specially beautiful plumage and short feathers, as well
as with divers, and aquatic birds, it is often desirable
to make the incision under the wing.   The great object
is to get the body out of the skin in the cleanliest
fashion, and so that none of the internal grease or juices
soil the plumage.   The overwhelming advantage then
of a neat operation, so that the body remain practically
unbroken, will be apparent at once.   Sometimes it
may be desirable to take the body out through the
back, when the incision is made in the same manner
as it would be on the breast.   In fact the features to
be specially preserved will rule the operator's choice in
this respect.   I, however, now suppose that the cut is
made from the breast-bone as seen in the illustration.

Now put down the knife, and use the hands only, for the fingers are the best instruments. Insert the fingers under the skin on one side, and clear the skin

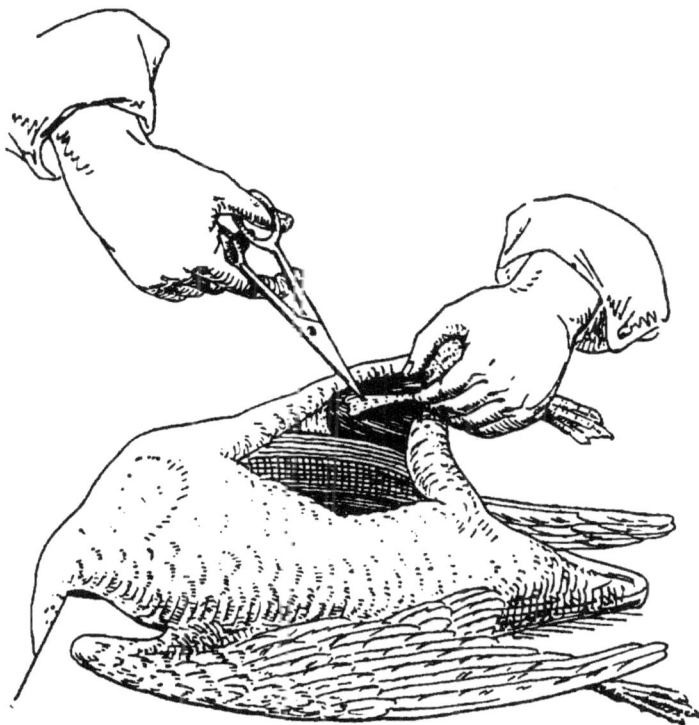

from the flesh in all accessible parts. That done, insert below the skin a sufficient quantity of dry plaster of Paris, or such other similar material as, wanting plaster of Paris, you may be compelled to use to absorb such blood or other moisture as may at the moment be present. Treat the corresponding side in like manner. Next proceed to force out the leg. In order to do this, hold the leg firmly above the joint, and force the thigh through the aperture, at the same time carefully drawing off the skin; insert the point of the scissors below the flesh next the bone, and

move them skilfully up between the bone and muscle,
until, by raising the right hand a little, the scissors can
be made to nip the bone transversely just against the
joint; cut the bone through and you can then thrust

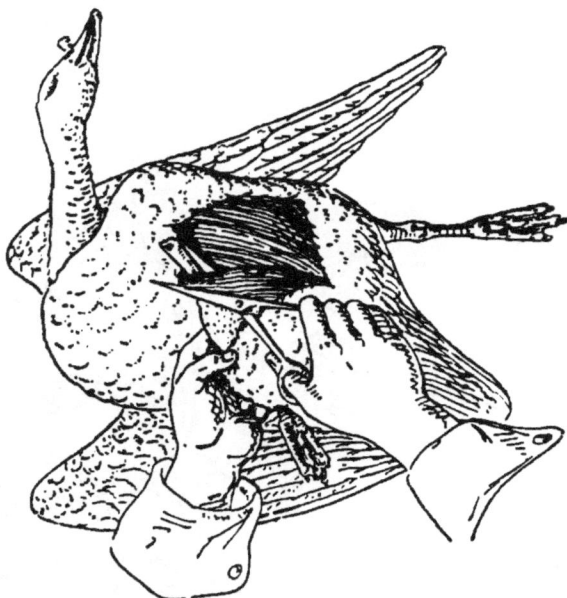

it out naked from the flesh, and with the scissors cut
the tendons next the *tarsus,* and the whole muscle of
the thigh will come away in one piece, leaving the

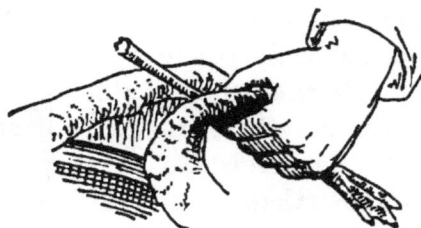

bone clean. This bone
must be cut near the
femur joint, leaving
the head of the bone
which is useless with
the flesh attached to
the thigh and body.
The bone, when thus freed, should appear as above.
Having treated both legs thus, skin up to the root of the
tail, but in severing the *vertebræ* leave the whole triangular projection in which the feathers are imbedded

for after treatment. It is a common error to cut this portion too low down, and much trouble results. Now

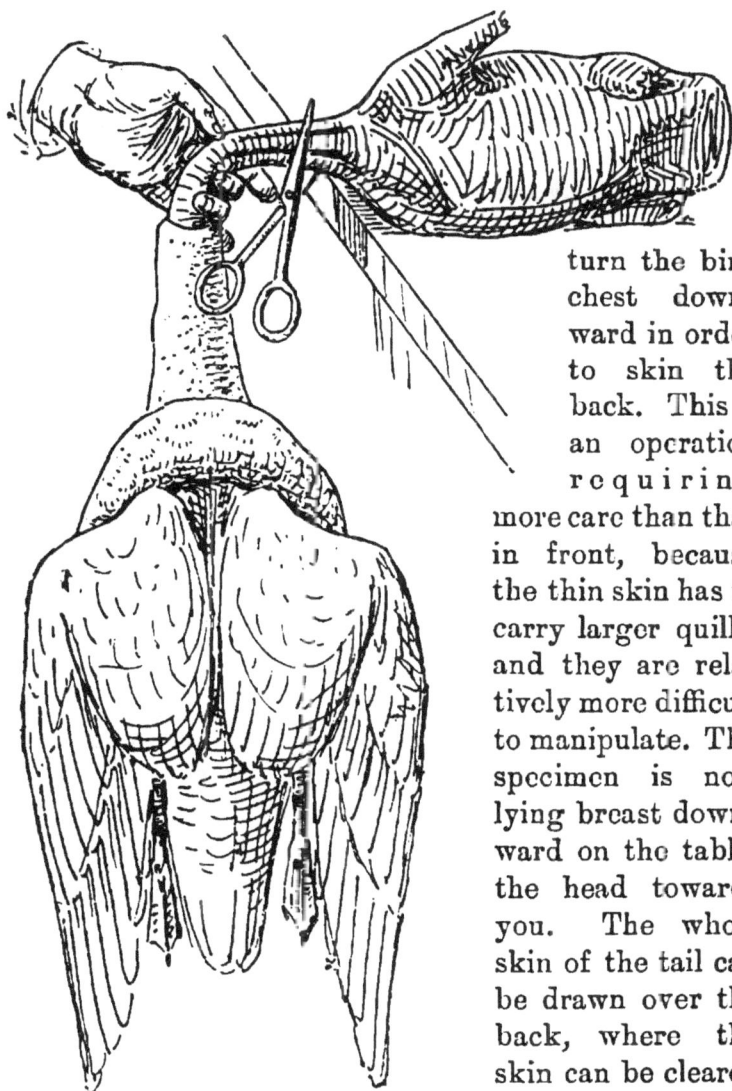

turn the bird chest down-ward in order to skin the back. This is an operation requiring more care than that in front, because the thin skin has to carry larger quills, and they are rela-tively more difficult to manipulate. The specimen is now lying breast down-ward on the table, the head towards you. The whole skin of the tail can be drawn over the back, where the skin can be cleared by the blunt side of the scalpel, and the body will thus be freed down to the wings. Here free the body by cutting the flesh through with the scissors at the point of fracture of the *humerus*, and thereupon free the whole body from the skin until only the neck remains to be severed, as shown in the illustration.

The next step is one requiring judgment and dexterity. The head must be got away. With ducks, geese, and similar birds, the head is too large to come through the neck-skin, and, in such cases, an opening must be neatly made from the back of the head, about two inches down the neck, of sufficient size to admit of the skull being removed for cleaning. Through this orifice force the skull, skinning it carefully until past the eyes, and in doing this pay particular attention not to work any injury to the

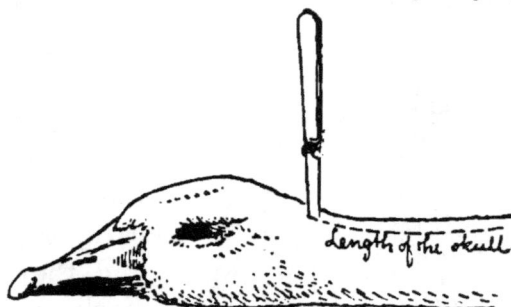

Length of the skull

edges of the eyes, or to the ears; these last should not be rudely touched by the knife. Cut away the back part of the skull, with neck, tongue, and palate. Remove the brains and the eyes. The whole skin is then in a condition to be cleaned and prepared. The first thing to do now is to take away all fat and flesh, and make your skin as cleanly as you can; then dress the inside with arsenical soap. Bind some tow round the leg-bones where the muscle was, and restore them to their proper position. Put some cotton-wool in place of the eyes, and, having forced some of the arsenical soap into the skull, return it to its place. In the case of the large birds—the specimen figured in our illustrations is a goose—the wing must be treated thus: Open the skin from the outside along the bones as shown below, removing the muscle, without disturbing the hold of the feathers on the bone; the quills here join the bone. It is important to bear this in mind, for if a serious error be made here the wing will be shapeless. Small birds can be treated from the inside. It is not desirable to use powdered alum to bird-skins,

as it tends to make them brittle. The specimen should then be filled out by stuffing to the natural size, and a band of paper placed round it in order to keep the wings and other parts in proper position till dry. During the whole operation, wood dust, or other dry powder should be freely employed to absorb blood and grease, so that the plumage may be kept clean.

When the skin of a specimen has been taken off in manner set forth above, there is a proceeding which it is important to observe, that is called technically "making the skin." This is in reality a part of the operation of skinning, indeed that part of it which consists in finishing the work in a workmanlike manner. While the skin is fresh and supple it must be so disposed that as it dries it may take proper form rather than distortion, and much after-trouble will be saved. The skin, as it is inside out, must be cleaned—this is indispensable—and the arsenical soap properly applied. Directly that is done, it is well to sprinkle the surface of the soap with some dry powder—say plaster of Paris, so that in handling the adhesiveness of the paste may not be inconvenient. It will be noticed that the skin between the wings, when raised from the bony structure, exhibits among the quills certain bare places. Now these would be most unsightly if they appeared prominent on the finished specimen. The tendency of the hollow skin, at this part especially, is to be too large, and it is better for after-operations that the skin should rather be contracted that expanded to anything approaching looseness. In setting up the bird, it is far easier to stretch the skin, if required, than to contract it; and now is the time to catch up and stow away any seemingly superfluous folds. These are most conspicuous on the back. To get rid of them, tie the wing-bones inside with a thread that shall lie across the back, and draw the wings together as near as in judgment they may best represent the position in life. This will enable the feathers to cover in the naked skin, that would otherwise appear, and will give solidity, so to speak, to the plumage at this part. This is little present trouble, but is the saving of infinite trouble in the future, and is of great consequence for the beauty of the bird. Having done this, turn the plumage out, but be careful in doing so not to fracture the skin of the neck. Use the scissor-forceps to fill in the neck with cut tow; fill in the body; smooth the feathers into proper position, and your whole bird into proper shape. Place a paper band round the wings, that they may set in good position. Small birds can conveniently be slipped into a cone of paper.

It may sometimes fall to the lot of the traveller to secure an albatross, and at the same time he may not always know what to do best with his unwieldy and not very rare specimen. If he does not care to preserve it whole, he may well be reminded that there are some parts of it which may be profitably saved. The long tubular wing-bones are prized for pipe-stems, to which they can be adapted well; the great web-feet will make beautiful tobacco pouches when properly prepared, or a curious small work-bag for a lady can be formed of the same trophies. The wing-bones must be carefully cleaned: a good way is to open the orifice at each end, and boil them; or they can be macerated in water. The foot should be treated thus : sever the bone above the knee; cut the skin down the back of the shank and heel; insert the thumb and finger—you must not use any sharp instrument—so as to separate the web on both sides from the bony structure of the toes ; do this down to the outer talons, and so that the toes can be drawn out of the web-pouch now formed; sever the talons from the bones on the inside with the scissors, leaving the talons attached outside ; clean the skin neatly, and dress it well with arsenical paste ; fill the pouch with wool, or tow, or sawdust, to keep it in shape. Of course the utilisation of parts of birds and animals in this way is mainly a question of inventiveness and

ingenuity, for many natural features may be adapted
to the most useful and ornamental purposes, while at
the same time they retain the character of trophies.
The leg-bones of the Flamingo are long and have
an elegant curve—they will form admirable pipe-
stems; the teeth of animals can be adapted orna-
mentally in many ways; the talons of a tiger, or the
hoof of an antelope, or the tusk of a boar, may, as
well as antlers and more pretentious features, be
employed for adornment or use; and there is just
this advantage, that they may in some circumstances
be saved, when the whole trophy has to be abandoned.

Birds can be kept in spirit, and this mode is
particularly useful for the preservation of young birds
in the down, very small specimens, etc.

REPTILES AND FISH.—As a general rule large specimens are skinned and preserved in similar manner to
birds, although with reptiles alum may be used, especially on the thicker portions of the skin; but small
specimens are kept in spirit. It must rest with the
traveller himself to determine which course is best for
saving the particular example he has secured. When a
fish is skinned whole, he must be laid out carefully on
a board, and the incision must be made not down the
belly but along the centre of the least important side,
from gill to tail. The object is to remove the body
from the skin, with the least possible disturbance of
the scales, etc. The skin can be manipulated neatly
from each side of the incision. When, in this operation, you come to the base of fins, cut the obstruction
inside the skin with the scissors, but with judgment,
so as not to sever them too closely, that they may not
be unsettled. Cut in like manner the *vertebræ* next
the base of the head, and next the extremity of the

tail; then, if need be, cut them also in the middle so
that the flesh may be taken away in two pieces; but
this is a matter of convenience, and must be made to
subserve the all-important point of not disturbing,
bending, or otherwise injuring the skin, for the scales
that constitute the characteristic beauty to be preserved are very fragile and easily detached, and to
break or detach them is fatal to the value of the
specimen. Clean the head as well as you can, and
then paint the whole interior surface of the skin with
arsenical paste and apply the same preservative to the
head, into the cavities of which cotton wool may be

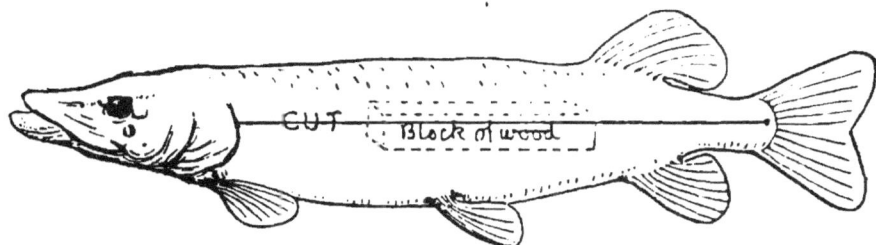

pushed. The body should be filled with dry sawdust
up to its natural shape; next draw the edges of the
orifice together with neat stitches. The fins and tail
must then be treated. These, while wet and pliant,
must be set out in natural form on pieces of card, so
that they may dry as they are intended to be displayed.
The specimen can now be put on one side to dry.

This process, however, rather presupposes the
opportunity for quiet treatment at home. When the
naturalist is on the field, shorter means may be used.
The skin being removed and dressed with arsenical
soap, may be left to dry in convenient form. The
skins can then be packed together, and it will be
found useful to pack with them some light stiff

material like thin wood, dried rushes, etc., that disposed longitudinally will prevent the possibility of the brittle skins being bent accidentally.

The smaller fish and reptiles, when preserved in spirit, should be saved in form as uninjured as possible. Carefully preserve the natural appearance of the creature so far as may be; and it is very important that on a label (of tinfoil or paper) attached to the specimen itself, or to the receptacle wherein it is placed, should be noted a sufficient description of it made at the moment it is fresh before you, especially

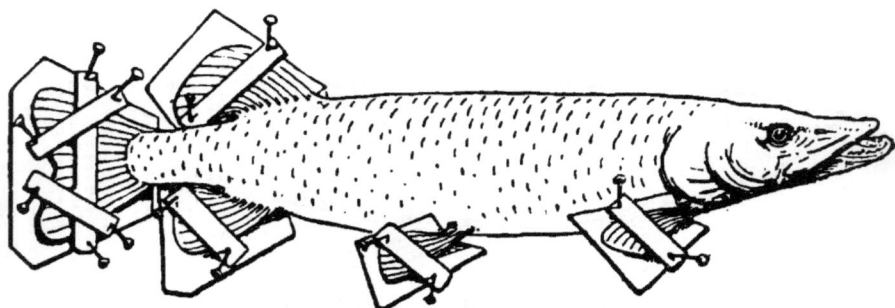

of colours and appearances and features which may disappear or be altered by the spirit, unless the species be quite well known and these details are manifestly unnecessary. Be particular as to the locality in which the specimen has been captured.

INSECTS.—The ingenuity displayed by the collector in capturing and storing insects is often a personal quality, and the methods that may be adopted are almost infinite. The general methods most approved are all that can be referred to here. Butterflies, moths, and some other species, whose beauty is in their colouring and is very fragile to the touch, must be treated for storage and preservation in a different

way from beetles and insects of similar class. In fact,
all excepting the first named may be preserved in
spirit so soon as captured for after treatment, and
they need not be injured by the process. For
permanent display in the cabinet, all insects must
be properly set out—the *Lepidoptera* with distended
wings, and the Coleopterous insects in suitable position. They should be killed the instant they are
captured, to prevent injury resulting from efforts to
escape. A gauze net is generally used. When a
butterfly is got into it, the collector watches his opportunity while the insect is still in the gauze, and so
soon as it closes its wings he lightly and sufficiently
pinches its thorax between his thumb and finger. The
butterfly falls from the net dead and uninjured. The
specimen must not be handled excepting to pick him
up by the legs, holding which the wings may be slightly
blown apart and a proper pin pushed through the
body, so that the specimen with closed wings may
at once be stored in the collecting box, or if the
creature be not quite dead the pin can be inserted on
the under part of the cork in the cyanide bottle, and
the specimen kept there till dead. Butterflies should
be stored thus with folded wings, until they are required to be set out for the cabinet. When the collector reaches home, he can store the contents of his
pocket box, by putting each specimen in a small
triangular envelope of paper, outside which a note
may be made. Hundreds can be stored in small space.
Moths, on account of their greater rotundity, must
not be treated in exactly the same manner by pinching.
They are not frequently captured in the gauze, and
are best killed in the cyanide bottle, or by the application of a little prussic acid. They are conveniently

taken home in separate pill-boxes.   Beetles, etc., may
as a rule be well preserved in spirit, which kills them
forthwith ; or they can be killed in the cyanide bottle.
When the time arrives for arranging insects for the
cabinet, the Butterflies can be relaxed by placing them
for a time on wetted sand, or exposing them to steam.
The wings, legs, etc., can then easily be set out by
the aid of small pieces of card on pins (see figs. E, F).
Beetles, etc., should be set out while they are wet when
taken from the spirit (see p. 26 as to preservatives).

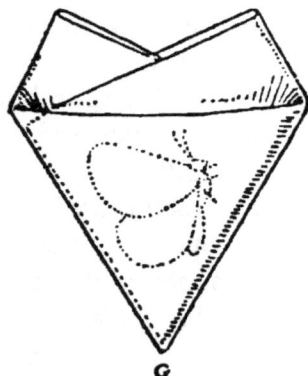

G

     In England, and on the Continent of Europe, many
entomologists now study the exotic species, which they
can obtain from friends or correspondents residing
abroad, either in the *ovum* or egg state, or in the
chrysalis or pupa state.   Most people know that from
the eggs (*ova*) of Butterflies and Moths come out
caterpillars or *larvæ*.   These *larvæ* moult several
times, and after each moult, in some species, there is
a remarkable change in the colour of the *larva*.   The
larvæ of many species of *Lepidoptera* go into the
ground to change into the *pupa* state, and sometimes
they form a shell in the ground ; some turn into *pupæ*

in leaves, others on the ground in a sort of web. The
pupæ of Butterflies are most often found on grasses,
twigs of shrubs, or on trees; others on walls or
fences.

The *pupæ* of many species of *Bombyces* are in-
closed in cocoons most often found on trunks, and
especially on branches of trees. Some of these cocoons
are remarkable by their size and the beauty of their
silk. When the leaves of the trees have fallen, these
cocoons are easily seen hanging from the branches.

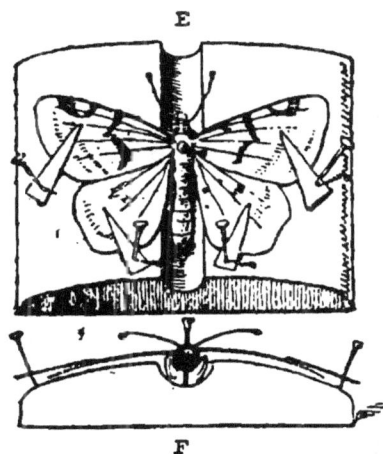

In some species of *Lepidoptera*, the *imagines* (perfect
insects), male and female, are very much alike, but the
body of the ♂ is larger than that of the ♀. The
Moths of the male *Bombyces* have *antennæ* (horns)
very much more pectinated than those of the female;
the body of the latter also is generally much larger.
Persons wishing to rear the *larvæ* should keep the
Moths in cages, in order that the eggs may be secured.

With respect to the rearing of the *larvæ* of large
Bombyces, the following plan may be adopted, till the
second or third stage. Use large bell-glasses, with a

few holes in the dome, or glasses open at the top, which in this case must be covered with gauze. Place these glasses on saucers full of sand covered with a piece of paper. Through the paper stick into the sand some branches of the food plants proper to each species. Place the young *larvæ* on these. Under bell-glasses, which, of course, must be placed in the shade, no water is required to keep the little branches fresh, and the young *larvæ*, which are apt to wander till the first or second moult, cannot escape. When the *larvæ* are large, it is best to rear them on large branches plunged in water, and without the glass covering. This refers to the rearing of the large silk-producing *Bombyces*, and of all those forming some sort of cocoon. When the *larvæ* have to bury themselves to change into *pupæ*, it is of course necessary to rear them in a box, containing a few inches of mould. This method should always be adopted when the habit of the *larvæ* is not known. Breeding cages, which, as a rule, should always be large, must have their sides of perforated zinc to give air. Cages ought to open by the middle, like two boxes open on one side, and placed one over the other, and fastened by hinges.

When *pupæ* have to be sent to England from very distant countries, especially if they have to cross the tropics, they can be conveniently transmitted in small strong boxes by sample post; each box not to exceed eight ounces, and to be registered, but place the stamp where the stamping will do no harm. The *pupæ* should be sent as soon as they are formed; and if underground *pupæ* they should be placed in soft damp moss. The boxes should also have a few holes in the sides to admit air.

If boxes containing *pupæ* or *ova* of *Lepidoptera*

could be placed in the ice-house on board ship, which would retard considerably the emergence of the Butter-flies or Moths and the hatching of the eggs, valuable species could be sent from very distant countries. Salmon *ova* were thus safely forwarded from England to Australia and Tasmania.

ARTISTIC SETTING-UP OF TROPHIES.

In order to reproduce the life-like form of any animal by the employment of its preserved natural features, not only technical skill, but knowledge and artistic feeling are necessary to the production of a worthy work. Formerly, the process aptly termed "stuffing" was employed. The results were seldom or never of more that a relative value, especially in regard to the mammalia. The fact was too often ignored that the use of astringents, necessary to preserve a skin, in-variably distort it, that this distortion differs even in several parts of the same skin, by reason of the varying thickness or even the condition of health in which the animal was killed; for instance, the skin of a fat animal is liable to undue expansion, that of a poor beast, to peculiar contraction; and mere stuffing can give only an untrue representation of the living creature. It is therefore incumbent upon the operator, firstly, to make himself thoroughly acquainted with the habits of the animal in a state of nature; and next to choose some incident of the creature's living existence which he desires his specimen to illustrate. This will enable him to arrive at his design. He must then make himself acquainted not only with the bony but the muscular structure of the animal, by which knowledge he can, if he have the proper technical and artistic skill, produce a *model*, whereon he can properly place the skin and other natural features of the specimen, so as to make as perfect a representation as practicable of the living animal, in form and detail, and of the creature's living habits in his design. This is the only course whereby noble trophies can be made to have more value than a paper description of them would possess. On the individual skill, knowledge, and taste of the artist depends the real value of the work,—in the same way as that of the sculptor, or painter, is in degree to be estimated.

A typical animal to illustrate the propositions laid down above is the Tiger, because of his various and picturesque habits, his magnificent proportions, and great beauty. I shall, therefore, describe the setting-up of a specimen of this feline in detail. But here a qualifying observation must be made. No book description can adequately convey all that should be known. To learn what is necessary the personal instruction of a good teacher, and the smallest modicum of experience, is worth more than any printed course of instruction, however ostensibly complete. We will, then, suppose that a perfect skin, in good condition, has been procured. Let us select the simplest action of the creature, viz., his stealthy walk through a grassy jungle, which is his habitat, when his peculiar expression is that of constant caution, whether he be in retreat, or advancing, with the snarl of ready offence which is habitual with him. This is the design. As digitigrade quadrupeds, the cats walk on their toes, and the claws then being retractile are concealed. The left hind leg and the right fore leg, or *vice versâ*, are used together in progression. There is a difference in

the pose of the ear to express alertness, caution, or
anger. In the first case the ear is erected; the ear is
partially depressed when the beast is only cautious,
but in anger, or incipient anger and alarm, the ear is
levelled with the skin of the head. We will choose
the semi-depression. The mouth should be partially
open, showing the teeth and tongue, but the lip not
raised, the expression being that of slightly panting.
In order to produce this design, first study the skin
and form a judgment of its natural dimensions, as to
height, bulk, etc. A distinct preparation of the skin
is necessary as a preliminary to this. It must be what
is technically called "shaved" or "fleshed." This
process consists in first softening the raw skin—which
is most often native-dressed with lime—by sponging
the flesh plentifully with liquor. The skin is then
placed on a rounded beam conveniently, and what is
termed the "pelt"—the *enderma*, in fact—is removed,
by scraping and shaving, with a currier's knife, the
edge of which is turned peculiarly for the purpose.
This, in reducing the substance of the skin, renders it
elastic and better adapted for use on the model, which
must be now constructed. The head, with the lips,
eyes, and burrs of the ears, as well as the feet, must
be carefully shaved with an ordinary knife, skilfully
manipulated. Now fold over the skin with the hair
outwards, so that the limbs accord with the intended
position; measure the points and make the best estimate possible under the conditions as to bulk, etc. The
limbs should be folded and the whole arranged as nearly
as may be to give the outline of the animal.

In making the model first deal with the trunk.
Two 1½-inch boards, 11 inches wide, of proper length,
should be glued, and what carpenters term "dowalled"

together by the edges. Place the skin as folded to represent the animal flat on this board, and from it draw thereon the outline of the trunk. Cut the board to this outline—to the inside of it, so that room be allowed for the modelling of the muscles on this framework. Get four sufficient iron rods—⅜-inch is the medium gauge—for the legs, one for the tail, and two to support the head. Bore a hole through the board where the *scapula* or blade-bone would come. Through this pass the rod till about 15 inches are on

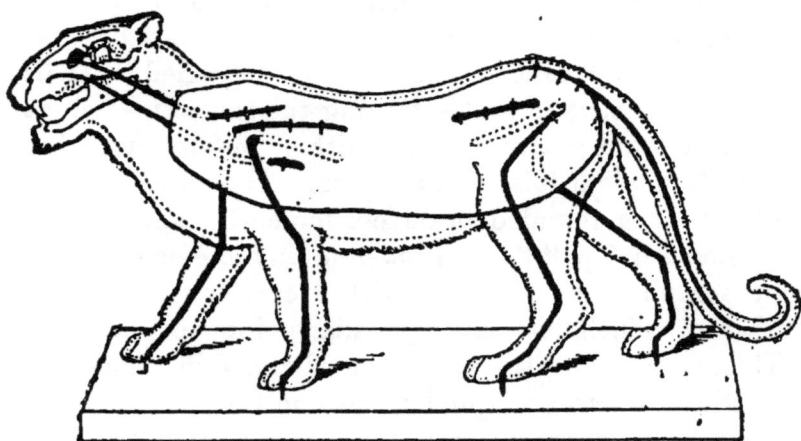

the other side, then bend this portion sharp round at right angles, to be fastened by staples firmly along the board in the direction of the hind quarter. At about 3 inches from the board bend the rod again, and incline it forward at such an angle as represents the natural position of the *scapula*; then bend the rod back again for the *humerus*, and once more forward for the *ulna* and *radius*, then shortly for the carpal and metacarpal bones. This is the extent of the rod, which must now be taken through a wooden stand and fastened under it. It will be seen that this iron, which must be repeated exactly on the other side, is intended to take the place of the absent bones, and that it must stand away from the board just such distance as the original bones would have occupied. The hind legs should be treated in similar manner (see diagram). The iron for the tail must be appropriately bent, and attached to the board in position; as also the two irons to support the skull, which must now be attached.

The next operation is to carve in soft wood the bones and muscles of the limbs, keeping them small enough to be finally covered with clay. I use a particular substance of my own invention for this modelling, and it dries as hard as marble without any shrinkage; it is never brittle. The first group, " The Combat," that I was able to produce by this means, was exhibited in the International Exhibition (1871), in Division III. (*Scientific Inventions and New Discoveries.*) The wood, representing bones, should be made in pieces, much as a lay figure is made. The pieces then being sawn through the centre longitudinally, a hollow space should be cut down them, not only to lighten them, but that they may be riveted together over the iron, so that the rod occupies the place, as it were, of marrow in the bone.

The trunk must be built up so as to be light and hollow, but with an appropriate surface to receive the clay. Behind the shoulder, midway, and next the thigh, should be fixed, on either side of the central board, segments of 1-inch board, of proportion sufficient to give the required bulk, and to secure the contour of the ribs, etc. A nearly circular board must be shaped to distend the neck. Across the edges of these boards coarse, strong canvas must be neatly tacked, small laths being inserted at proper places to prevent the canvas sinking. The rod which is to support the tail must be covered with tow, neatly bound on to the required form, and then in like manner sewn up in the canvas. The same material must also be extended over the skull, whereon the fleshy excrescences must be represented cleverly by tow. We have thus a complete light framework covered with strong canvas, excepting the limbs. On all necessary places over the whole framework a surface of modelling clay is to be worked. The ribs and prominent muscles of the trunk, the muscular development of the shoulders and haunches, the joints and extremities, must all be carefully modelled on. Ordinary modelling clay is used; and when the model is finished, and nearly dry, paper should be pasted over the clay to prevent it from breaking away. A good method is to perfectly steep brown paper in a pailful of hot paste. The softened paper can be put in small pieces over the clay, and readily adheres.

The model is now completed and made ready to receive the natural features of the animal. First of all the eyes must be carefully adjusted in the most natural manner; the claws must be next inserted in position. It remains to place the skin. This must be again damped with liquor till quite soft, and in this state it must be carefully arranged on the model. First manipulate the head, paying particular attention to adjust the lips, eyelids, and ears properly, so that the required expression may be secured. It is advisable now to tack together the edges of the skin in certain places, as under the throat, the four joints under the armpits, and at the groin, midway under the belly, at intervals along the tail and the limbs. Adjust the soft skin to the inequalities of the model, using a "piercer" and the thumb. The seams must be carefully and neatly sewed up. A delicate and important operation remains. The skin should fit perfectly all the indentations of the model. In order to attain this, the skin, when worked wet into the recess, should be secured there wherever necessary by drawing pins, which must not be withdrawn until the model is perfectly dry. Then, the pins being removed, the fur can be cleansed in the usual way, viz.: rub with the hands very fine mahogany dust all over the coat; then beat it with a fine cane and finish with a brush. The tongue, which is modelled in clay, and tinted, should now be placed in the mouth, where the tinting can be finished. At the same time, the lips, eyes, and nose can be tinted and finished. The pigment used should be the finest tube oil colour. It is best before painting to cover the mucous surfaces with hot wax, which promotes the naturalness of the appearance most materially. The whiskers which may have come from the skin should be carefully replaced.

Accept it as a golden rule never to cut the skin.

The method described above is given on the presupposition that the skin is one as ordinarily received from India, cured by native practitioners. But in cases where the skeleton of a beast is preserved, and is available, much of the work may be saved by utilising the bones, especially for the limbs; and in any case they furnish the true proportions of the animal, which are so difficult for the inexperienced operator to arrive at without them.

The mounting of Head Trophies is best achieved in the following manner: If the head has been received in pickle, the skin should be thoroughly cleansed in fresh cold water, and should directly afterwards be shaved on the flesh side, as directed in the case of the tiger skin. Whether it be the head of a Tiger, a Stag, or a Bison, the process is the same. A proper estimate must be taken of the length of neck. What is called a neck-board must be prepared accordingly; that is a framework to which the skull is to be attached, and whereon the skin of the neck can be distended properly. This board is a flat piece of inch deal, 11 inches wide, cut to the shape of the neck, as the central board is shaped for the trunk of the tiger. The construction is on the same plan, the form being modelled in like manner. This neck-board is fixed to a heart-shaped back-board, by means of which it can be hung against a wall. The skull and horns having been firmly fixed on the artificial neck, the skin should be placed on the model and carefully adjusted. In well prepared trophies the seam should be up the nape of the neck, and the throat be intact. The nostrils, lips, and eyelids of the Stag, or Bison, should be moulded with artistic feeling and particular care, and clay should be injected between the mucous and outer skin of the lips, nostrils, and eyelids, so as to give them the rotund, fleshy appearance they have in life. It is better to insert the eye in its orbit before the skin is drawn on. The ears must be manipulated into shape while they are drying, and when the specimen is dry it can be cleaned in the usual manner.

Of small mammals the Squirrel will probably serve best as an example, and in this instance I shall presume that the skin has just been removed from the animal in a fresh condition, according to the method fully described on page 32. It is always an advantage to set up a skin while it is fresh. Prepare a body wire about 12 inches long, and of the thickness of ordinary whipcord; cover this with tow to the size of the carcase that has been removed, and bind the tow neatly with hemp; in fact, shaping the tow as nearly as possible to represent the form of the squirrel. For a sitting position, bend the wire so that the artificial body have the necessary arch of the back. The end of the wire next the tail must be turned and concealed in the body. Certain stitches through with a long needle will assist materially in shaping the form and strengthening the frame. A wire covered with the requisite quantity of tow will form the tail. Four wires, each about 8 inches long, will be required for the limbs. Pass these wires severally through the fleshy pad of the extremities, and bind the bones to the wire with cotton, taking care to leave about 2 inches of wire beyond the *humerus* and *femur*, so that they may be passed into the frame of the body and clinched. Next fill out each limb by carefully binding tow in proper proportion round the bone. Never exceed the natural size. The bones having been returned to the skin and the limbs completed, the upper end of the body wire should be cut so as to protrude only 1 inch and then should be inserted in the skull, the whole skin meanwhile being turned over the skull. A stitch driven through from eye to eye will fasten the head securely to the artificial neck. Small portions of tow must be inserted where the flesh has been taken from the skull, which can then be returned and the skin drawn into its position. The limb wires can now be inserted in the body and clinched. The skin having been properly drawn over, the parts can be neatly sewed up, the limbs bent to their natural position, and the wires of the feet passed through a stand so as to

be secure. It will be found advisable to manipulate
the skin with the "piercer" and thumb, in order
neatly to adjust it, and finish the specimen to taste.
The eyes should next be inserted by adhesive glue paste.
The fur should not be cleaned till the skin is quite dry.

Reptiles may be treated in precisely the same
manner.

Birds, when the skin has been properly removed
and dressed, as directed on pages 36–45, should be set

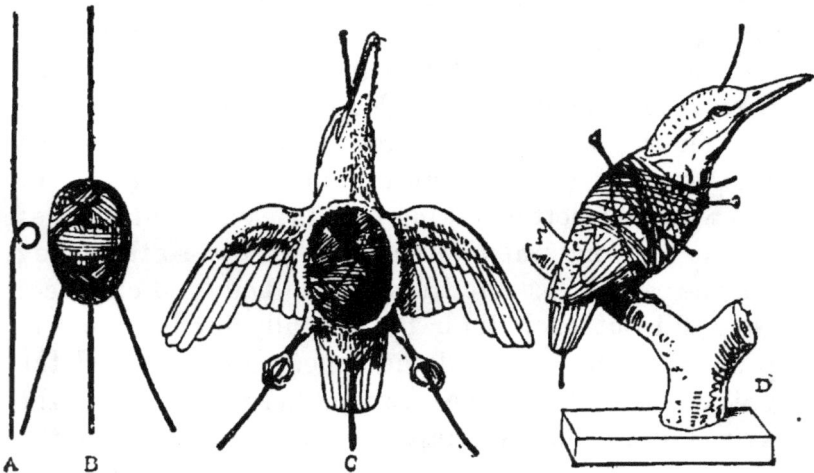

A   B   C   D

up in manner following. For example, a Pheasant, say
freshly skinned, should have a similar body wire to
that employed for the Squirrel, but proportionately
stouter to sustain the extra weight. The leg wires
should be half as stout again as the body wire, and
should be inserted at the back of the *tarsus* where the
tendon runs. The fleshy part of the thigh must be
made up in the same manner as directed in the case of
the Squirrel, while the body and neck is to be formed
on the body wire (see fig. A) in precisely the same
way. In the illustration, fig. A is the body wire;

fig. B is the same dressed neatly with tow bound with
thread to the size of the bird's body; similar wire must
be appropriately dressed for a long-necked bird. With
most birds the neck is almost hidden by the feathers;
but some species have necks (like the Heron) requiring
special treatment. With the last named the substance
is formed on the wire. With the first mentioned but
little stuffing is needed, and that can be loosely inserted before the wire, which may be pushed through
it. One end of this body wire is thrust up the neck
and right through the skull, so that it appear right
through the top; while the other end is made to protrude from the other extremity to support the tail.
The leg wires must be inserted through the sole of the
foot and under the skin up the back of the leg where
the tendon was, until the pointed wire is worked between the thumb and finger to equal position with
the thigh-bone; push this bone with the wire through,
bind both with the requisite tow, and draw them back
into the skin of the thigh, then continue working the
wire on, until it has progressed enough to pierce right
through the tow on the body wire. The leg wires
must cross, and where they cross in the body they
must be firmly twisted together with the pliers, so that
the junction is covered by the tow. Much depends
on the firmness of this fastening. Next insert such
wool as may seem necessary to fill out the breast, and
sew the skin neatly up. Dress the feathers smooth
and bend your bird into shape, next wire him on to
his perch, or other stand, and so you gain use of both
hands. Place a short wire through the quills of the
tail to spread the feathers. Set the wings into position with wires, and insert a pin wire into the back,
another into the breast; then, by means of these,

lightly baste the specimen with cotton so that the feathers may dry in proper position. The symmetry and natural pose of the specimen should be a matter of most careful study. No amount of technical skill, or of imaginative power, will in the least compensate truly for the knowledge of nature. To have seen the bird healthy in his natural habitat, and to be able to reproduce his natural behaviour and appearance, is an inestimable advantage. We cannot all of us command that; but we can do the next best thing, rely on the information communicated by others who have. My late father, when travelling with Audubon, accumulated an inestimably valuable store of such information; for it was the invariable practice, of that great naturalist directly a specimen was secured, and before any treatment of it, to have a sketch made of it, in the carefully observed natural position of life, with record of all colours and contiguous, or surrounding, natural features. Nothing is worse than to give a pretended character to a specimen, or to mount it with details that are anachronisms—such as to put ferns and grasses with birds who never existed where such ferns or grasses grew; or, to put seaweeds with creatures who do not frequent the ocean or sea-shore. The true sportsman-naturalist should esteem the record of an animal's pose or habits in life as important as any other record, so that when the specimen comes to skilled treatment, the naturalness of it may be a feature that enhances its value in every way. The line of form in many animals is not given by the skin, but by the fur, or feathers, as the case may be. He spoils a restored specimen who destroys this character by too much smoothing. By the eye and erection of the fur, the expression of anger is given. Some birds have the power of erecting their feathers, their crests, or position of their plumage, in token of passion, or for purposes of cleaning their plumes, as when a Pelican emerges from the water; and all character is destroyed by the misapplication of neatness, by too much tying down of feathers, or purposeless stroking of the fur. A test of proper treatment is the setting-up of the neck. Too frequently the neck is quite distorted by the stuffing, and elongated out of all proportion in the finish. The carriage of the head in nature is of paramount expression. When a bird is dead the muscles of the neck become flaccid, and the neck seems to be longer. This tendency is often aggravated by unskilful treatment of the skin, and destructive disproportion may result. It is a fault to guard against, and an arrangement to be carefully achieved. For instance, a Duck, sitting on the water, shows but little length of neck; sometimes, when at rest, hardly any; but the same bird in flight shows a long neck. Some knowledge of drawing and of modelling, seems to me to be essential to artistic setting-up of animals; and the best of specimens, inartistically mounted, are relatively worthless.

All the wire used for these operations should be annealed iron wire.

The dried skins of foreign birds must be softened and thoroughly relaxed before being manipulated for setting up. This is best effected by placing the specimen in a closed box, on wetted white sand, covered by paper, so that the evaporation may penetrate it. The duration of this process must be determined by the size of the bird; one night is sufficient for small

F

skins. The necessary stretching of the shoulders and other folded parts must be effected carefully, so as to assimilate the specimen to a green skin.

The grouping and "fitting-up," as the ornamentation is technically called, of specimens is an important point, and one the careful attention to which greatly enhances their value even in a museum, where such work is not ordinarily employed. Such addition to the naturalness of the subject often affords opportunity of, by little things, illustrating the habits and habitat of the animals. To take a pheasant, for example: Having set up the specimen, if it is intended to cover it by a glass case, a few natural ferns, suitable to the habitat of the bird, should be dried, and the faded colour restored, where necessary, by tinting with oil pigment. Grasses should be treated in the same way. The surface of the structure on which the bird is mounted—or, in other words, the ground—should be formed of calico, tacked with taste over a wooden framework to assume the required forms. It should then be covered with small pieces of brown paper that have been well soaked and softened in a mixture of glue and whiting. A few loose stones and portions of sand will readily adhere to this surface, and give the required reality of appearance. But it is necessary that these should not be applied until the surface is sufficiently hardened to receive them without being injured. An old root, pieces of lichen, and similar features can be introduced according to taste, so that they be accurately employed. The whole production must be painted with care, wherever painting may be necessary, so as to reproduce naturalness in the greatest perfection.

It is essential that the plumage of birds should be

quite clean and as perfect as possible before the specimen is mounted. The best way of removing blood
stains or other impurities from feathers is as follows:
Dissolve a piece of pure pipeclay, about the size of a
walnut, in a short pint of warm water, then with a
portion of fine flannel steeped in this liquid, and
soaped thoroughly with best yellow soap, saturate and
rub the feather the right way; having done this
sufficiently, immerse the feather, or the bird-skin, in
clear cold water till it is cleansed, then roll it in a
dry cloth, which, when duly pressed, will absorb the
water. Having done this, hold the specimen within
the heat of a fire, all the while beating it briskly and
lightly with the folded end of a clean towel. In the
case of detached feathers, they can be waved rapidly,
or swung round at the end of a string, before the fire.
Under this process plumage will resume its perfect
order. This is by far the most effective as well as
simplest operation of the kind, surpassing the employment of spirit and plaster of Paris, salts of sorrel, blue
water, etc.

A method of treating fish trophies must be mentioned here as being frequently more convenient, in
certain circumstances, than the skinning of them, and
at the same time sufficiently efficacious for the purpose.
This is to cast the specimen in plaster of Paris; and,
whether we care to complete the cast with imitative
colouring, or simply to preserve it in white, accuracy
of form is at least obtained. A mould must be made.
Most fish are more or less covered with a transparent
slime, which, for purposes of casting, would obscure
the small indications of form, such as scales, etc. This
coating must be got away. To effect this, lightly
sponge the specimen with dilute vitriol, which will

have the effect of changing the slime into an opaque film, which can be removed almost like a skin. The fish must then be carefully posed in position, on its side, and all those portions underneath the specimen where the plaster would penetrate should be filled in with clay; this, indeed, should form a bed for the fish, whose fins should be displayed on the surface by being impressed into it by means of the thumb. The plaster must be carefully prepared: put some water in a vessel and lightly shake the plaster, with the fingers, into it—not pour the water on to the plaster. The first batch should be very limpid, but little thicker than milk; it thickens rapidly as it stands. Pour this limpid plaster over the specimen—skilfully, so that each portion be well covered, and all the interstices filled with a first film of white. Directly this is set, put on a second coating of thicker plaster, and so on till the mould is thick enough; shape it at last roughly with the fingers. When dry, or rather quite hard, turn the mould over, pick out the clay, take out the fish, and the mould will be fit for use. This is what is called a "waste" mould, and the reason will be readily seen. The cast is produced by substituting plaster in place of the fish, thus: First dip the mould, if space admit of it, into clear cold water, so that the inner surface become thoroughly saturated; or, if the mould be too large to immerse it, wash the inside lightly over with sufficient clay-water, that is, water coloured with modelling clay; the object being by saturation to prevent all absorption on the inner surfaces. If the mould have been preserved till it is dry, an application of boiled oil will have the same effect. The plaster to be inserted must be skilfully mixed, at first quite limpid, and this must be washed

into the mould so as to fill all interstices, without any
bladders or bubbles appearing as this first coating sets.
A second coating strengthens the first, and so on;
but there is no occasion to make the object solid,
although the walls of the cast must be in all places of
sufficient thickness. When the plaster is well set hard,
the next process is to chip away the mould from the
cast, and the mould is therefore called "waste." This
requires skill in the application of sufficient, but not
too much strength. It is a convenient resource to
put a little tint into the plaster of the mould so that
it may be clearly distinguishable from the cast when
we come to chip it away. The cast when cleared should
present all details of the specimen perfectly. When
a number of copies of the cast is required it is necessary to make a "piece-mould"—a much more complex
operation. It is a mould that is made on the object,
in pieces that fit perfectly together and can be removed one by one from the cast, and replaced in position for each cast. It is necessary to make such a
mould on a cast, because the yielding nature of the
fish would bring about a distortion of parts in a piece-
mould; therefore a waste-mould must be employed in
the first operation. The piece-mould exercises the
skill of the operator and his judgment. No explanation
of the process could teach it so readily as the examination of the thing itself, and an old piece-mould can
easily be obtained in London, or similar cities, and this
resource of casting is not likely to be employed where
such a thing is not obtainable.

SKIN DRESSING.—It is a standing difficulty with
many sportsmen how best to prepare the skins of
animals, so as to make of them the supple and beautiful leather that leaves the hands of the professional

furrier; and thus to make the skins available for wearing apparel, rugs, etc., worked according to taste. The right way to proceed is the following: Let us suppose the subject to be the dried skin of an Indian Leopard. The skin must first be sponged on the flesh side with "liquor" till it is softened, and then it must be properly "shaved." It must then be partially dried. When in this condition the skin should be folded with the hair inwards, and the edges should be fastened together with stitches at intervals of about 12 inches. The object of this is, that the operator may subject the flesh side to the action of grease. For a Leopard, about 3 lbs. of lard will be required; this is the proper grease: butter turns rancid in the skin, and therefore must not be used. The usual mode is to put the skin into a clean tub with the grease, and to tread or knead it with the naked feet, till the action and the natural heat have caused the fat sufficiently and equally to penetrate the fibre of the pelt. The skin may then be laid open and "shaved" a little thinner on the flesh side. The next operation is to clean the fur. To do this, place the skin on a bench with the hair uppermost, and cover it well with fine mahogany dust procured from a veneer mill. Rub this powder with the hand well into the fur, so that it absorb all the grease, and at the same time it will cleanse the coat; and after the skin has been sharply beaten with light canes until the dust has all been removed, the natural brilliancy of the specimen will be restored. A process perhaps more convenient to many persons, but not so effectual, is to rub the grease in with the hand.

HUNTING FIELDS OF THE WORLD.

FOLLOWING are memoranda concerning some of the principal regions of the world which can be resorted to for big game, and where natural historical trophies of interest and value may be collected with advantage, while noble sport is pursued. It must, however, be borne in mind, that in almost every sparsely peopled country, and in many untrodden districts and islands not alluded to here, the study of natural history can be followed by collecting examples, or even specimens of new species and varieties, with absorbing interest and to the aggrandisement of science. The range of such fields is almost inexhaustible: and it includes countries, the fauna and other natural productions of which are imperfectly known to European naturalists, because (as may be said of the Chinese empire), they have been hitherto almost unvisited by them in a scientific sense. No attempt is made to give anything like a complete list of the animals to be found in any particular resort, but simply to supply some information of those most likely to be encountered, which may serve as an indication to the enterprising hunter.

SCANDINAVIA AND THE NORTH.—The accessibility of these grounds from England, the general healthiness

of tho climate, and certain conveniences of transit,
etc., which can bo commanded, recommend them.   In
Denmark Proper thero are none of the larger or
important *carnivora*.   Sweden and Norway, however,
which occupy tho peninsula, in their groat mountains
and forests afford retreat for several animals of interest, as well as for numberless game and raptorial
birds.   There aro many water-fowl.   In fact, this is a
breeding ground for hosts of the European birds, who
migrato thence, and are familiar elsewhere at certain
seasons.   The fishing, both freshwater and marine, is
very good, especially for salmon.   Many of the best
salmon rivers in Norway are now leased to English
sportsmen.   Snow covers the ground during seven
months of the year, and this gives a peculiar character
to much of the sport.   Formerly the predatory animals
were very numerous and destructive; they are plentiful
still, but are now confined principally to the northern
forests and the mountains.*   The inhabitants of in-
fested districts protect their cattle by general hunts
or battues, and by many ingenious systems of snaring.
The Brown Bear (*Ursus Arctos*), the largest and most
formidable of the Scandinavian *carnivora*, is seldom
encountered save in Dalecarlia and tho northern parts
of the peninsula.   This animal grows till he is twenty
years old, and is sometimes found of great size and
strength, weighing four or five hundredweight.
Wolves are to be found in plenty; the Glutton, or
Wolverine (*Ursus gulo*, Linn.), can be got in the forests

---

* A Swedish Government return shows that in 1827, throughout
thirty-four provinces, there were killed by beasts of prey, 35,548
head of horses, horned cattle, sheep, goats, pigs, etc., belonging to
farmers; and the estimated loss from this cause was in that year
£15,000.

of Dalecarlia, and more plentifully among the Lapland Alps farther north. Badgers. Foxes can be met with all over Scandinavia—the red, the black occasionally, and the Arctic white, mostly in the extreme north. There are, besides, Lynx, Marten, Weasel, Polecat, Ermine, Otter, etc. The noblest of the animals is probably the Elk, the largest of the *Cervidæ*; but, although protected, they are getting rare. In the province of Scania they were once numerous, but have now quite disappeared from there. The Reindeer is in like manner becoming scarcer, save in a domesticated condition; but these noble creatures may be still found wild in the Dalecarlian and Koelen mountains. There are also Red Deer and Roebuck. Of raptorial birds, the Golden Eagle will be found; and in Sweden only (and even there it has become scarce), the Great Bustard (*Otis tarda*, Linn.), the largest of European *Aves*. It used at one time to be common in Scania. It is sometimes, however, seen in Denmark. The Great Horned Owl (*Strix bubo*), and at the extreme north, in Lapland, the large Owl (*Strix Lapponica*), are to be found, as well as the Snowy Owl (*Strix nyclea*). The game birds are fine and plentiful. This is the head-quarters of the grouse genus. First among these is the Capercali, or Capercailzie (*Tetrao Urogallus*), the largest of the European *Gallinæ*. He is to be found in all the woods; in fact, wherever the pine tree flourishes, but best in the hilly districts. Those of the south weigh sometimes 16 lbs. or more; those captured in the north not so much. Blackcock (*Tetrao perdrix*, Linn.) are more numerous than the Capercali. Hazel-grouse (*Tetrao Bonasia*, Linn.) are abundant in the woods and on the hills of the northern parts. Ripas, both of the valley and

mountain species; the Dal Ripa (*Tetrao lagopus*, Linn.),
mostly in the northern wooded districts and on the
islands; and the Alpine Ripa (*Lagopus Alpina*)—by
some considered identical with the Scottish Ptarmigan
—which is mostly found on the Alpine ranges and on
the Norwegian islands; it haunts stone and shingle.
The common Partridge (*Perdix cinera*) is not very
plentiful. The Quail (*Perdix coturnix*) is to be met
with, but not numerously; it is migratory and rare,
especially in Sweden; there are a few in Norway.
The Woodcock (*Scolopax rusticula*, Linn.) is scarce,
and getting scarcer; these birds, however, are to be
met in considerable numbers, sometimes on the
western coasts at spring and fall; there are also
Snipe, etc. Aquatic birds are wondrously plentiful on
all the lakes and rivers. Fine shooting of this description is to be had in almost any part of Sweden or
Norway; but the best is probably at Nordholm.
Sport is good, too, on the Skärgard, or belt of islands.
Of the swimmers, the principal are—Swan, Goose,
Goosander, Merganser, Mallard, Teal, Golden Eye,
Tufted Duck, Widgeon, Long-tailed Hareld (*Harelda
glacialis*), Black-throated Diver, Red-throated Diver,
Great Black-backed Gull, Common Gull, Black Tern,
and Caspian Tern, etc. The scarce Steller's Western
Duck (*Anas dispar*) may be encountered, and should
be carefully looked for as a prize. Eider Duck is
found on the western coasts.

In the Arctic Sea.—Proceeding farther north,
remarkable sport is to be obtained amid the ice of the
Arctic Sea, by Spitzbergen, near Deeva Bay and
among the Thousand Islands, commencing in July.
Walrus or Sea Horse, and several species of the
valuable fur-bearing as well as common hair seals will

be met with. They must be harpooned as well as
shot; they are seldom killed by the gun unless they
are hit in the brain, which is at the back of what
appears as their head. Polar Bears (*Thalarctos maritimus*) may be encountered here. Polar Foxes and
Reindeer can be collected on shore. The Bears are
often of prodigious size and strength, sometimes, say,
8 ft. in length, 4 ft. 6 in. high at shoulder, and
weighing 1200 lbs. or more. Many large cetaceans are
in the sea; and sea-fowl are numerous.

RUSSIA.—Most of the species of animals and birds
inhabiting Sweden and Norway will be found in
northern Russia and Siberia; indeed, it may be said
that in some part or other of this vast empire all, or
nearly all the wild creatures native to Europe may be
found. Besides the great Brown Bear (*Ursus Arctos*),
another, the Siberian Bear (*Ursus collaris*), is to be
met with; the Musk Ox (*Ovibos Moschatus*) in the
high latitudes; and in the forest of Bialowicza, in
Lithuania, to the eastward of the Baltic, the mighty
Aurochs (*Bison priscus*), the ancient European Bison
of the Pliocene period. This last named wild bull,
one of the noblest of animals, more than 6 ft. high
at the shoulders, is very rarely to be got at, and is
rapidly becoming extinct. It is closely protected and
preserved for the private sport of the Czar and the
Imperial family. It exists also in certain districts of
Moldavia and Wallachia, and is found sparsely in some
parts of the Caucasus. There are plenty of Wolf,
Fox, Lynx, Otter, Sable, and other fur-bearing animals.
Of birds, there are several species of Eagles and other
Raptores not met with in Sweden and Norway.

THE MEDITERRANEAN AND ADRIATIC.—Particularly
for those who possess yachting advantages, the Medi-

terranean coasts and islands, as well as Dalmatia and Albania on the Adriatic, offer pleasant opportunities of sport, especially in regard to birds. Of mammals, the most notable is the Moufflon Sheep (*Ovis musimon*), to be had in the islands of Corsica, Sardinia, and (not so numerously) in Cyprus. The species in Sardinia is most esteemed by some hunters, as the ewes there are generally horned. In Corsica are plenty of wild Hogs, Stags, etc.; but in Greece and Turkey, as well as on the islands, there are many other mammalia of ordinary species. On the African coast, the Bush Goat or Barbary Deer (*Cervus Barbarus*) can be collected. Albania is a principal resort. The birds, especially waders and swimmers, are plentiful there and in many other parts. Some of the most noticeable are the following:—The Balearic Crane (*Balearica pavonina*), getting scarce; Rosy Flamingo (*Phœnicopterus ruber*, Linn.); Purple Waterhen; plenty of Snipe, Heron, Bittern, and other waders; Audouin's Gull, mostly about Corsica and Sicily; White-eyed Gull, among the Grecian Islands; Slender-billed Gull (*Larus tenuirostris*), especially on the African coasts; the Black-headed Gull is to be found in these seas, and especially in the marshes of Albania and Dalmatia, where it breeds. The Great Black-headed Gull, from the Caspian and Red Seas, is seen occasionally about the Ionian Islands; the Algerian Cinereous Shearwater (*Puffinus cinereus*, Cuv.). Sometimes, but rarely, and in hard weather, the Snow Goose comes from Northern Asia and America; and the Blue-winged Goose and the Little White-fronted Goose are found in Greece. The rare Marbled Duck can be got in Sardinia, and near Tunis in January and February; and it has been seen in the Ionian Islands. There

arc plenty of Cormorants. The White and the
Dalmatian Pelicans can be found all about Greece
and the Ionian Islands, on the borders of lakes
and rivers and in the swampy parts. There are
many fine species of the *Falconidæ* to be collected.
Francolin Partridge (*Tetrao francolinus,* Linn.) are to
be had in the Grecian Archipelago, Turkey, Sicily,
Malta, etc. ; and the *Perdix rufa.* The Greek Partridge
is getting scarce. The perching-birds are not greatly
dissimilar to the other European species; but among
them may be pointed out the Hoopoe, the Roller, the
Golden Oriole, and the Bee-eater.

ASIA.—The continent of Asia, of all divisions of
the globe, produces the most highly-developed forms
of the mammalia : nearly all of the higher animals are
to be met with there ; some are exclusively to be
found there. In the southern countries especially,
and in the islands of the Great Archipelago, toward
Australia, are some of the most remarkable hunting
grounds in the world.

INDIA.—This is perhaps the best field ; and, because
of the conditions of the British occupation, grand sport
can be had with seasonable convenience. Hunting is
an acknowledged resource, and means are attainable
in most places for pursuing it with success. In
Northern India the Himalayas divide Tibet from the
great plain of the Ganges. This range, because of
its very extent and the vastness of its features, is still
imperfectly explored. By reason of its position and
the great altitude of its mountains, it presents different
conditions of climate, with vegetation and fauna varying
in the most interesting ratio. Indeed, a double fauna
may be traced in these regions, namely, that which is
common to certain divisions of the mountains, and to

Tibet and Northern Asia ; and that which is common
to these hills, and the hilly regions of Assam and
Burmah, which are to the south of the eastern extremity
of this chain. Thus the variety of the game is most
remarkable, and each climatic zone has its characteristic
creatures. The mountains generally, and those districts
of the Gangetic Plains contiguous, furnish a grand
series of fine birds, and almost all the other animals
most prized by the sportsman in India, or perhaps in
the world. In the extreme north-west (Cashmere)
can be collected the Gigantic Sheep (*Ovis Ammon*), the
Burrell (*Ovis Nahura*), the Oorial (*Ovis cycloceros*),
the *Ovis Vignei*, the Ibex (*Capra Sibirica*), Markhor
(*C. megaceros*), four varieties, Tibetan Antelope (*Kemas
Hodgsonii*), Indian Antelope (*A. Bezoartica*), and some
of smaller species. Of *Cervidæ*, the grand Burra-
sing (*Cervus Cashmiriensis*) or Cashmere Stag, a very
fine species, frequenting the Saul Forests. The great
Shou Stag, a species larger than the Burra-sing, and
approaching the Wapiti in stature and magnificence of
antlers, is a fine trophy that will well repay the hunter.
But few specimens of this stag have as yet reached
England. The little Musk Deer (*Moschus moschiferus*),
etc. The Yak (*Bos grunniens*) may be got here, and
also at the other extremity of the chain in Bhootan.
Kyang, Wolf, Wild Dog, Lynx, Snow Bear, and Snow
Leopard are found here. At the foot of the hills, and
generally skirting the plain of the Ganges at this extremity, is a belt of swampy and densely-wooded
country in some places only three, in others fifty miles
wide, called the Terai, or marsh. This abounds with
numberless animals. Kumaon, the wonderful hill
district on the western edge of Nepaul, is nearly all
forest and Terai. Tigers are very numerous, Leopards,

many Bears, Spotted Deer (*Axis Maculata*), etc. Wild
Elephants are plentiful, especially in the rainy season,
and near where the land is cultivated. The Nepaulese
dominion, which lies along the Himalaya range, has
the Terai between it and the plains of Oude and
Behar. Almost parallel to this belt, but a few miles
further over the frontier, runs the great forest of
Nepaul. It is generally only about ten miles wide.
Therein are to be found plenty of Elephant, Rhinoceros
(*R. Indicus*), and Tiger. Thar (*Capricornis Bubalina*),
is a native of Nepaul, and is especially plentiful in the
eastern regions of that territory ; and only in the cold
upper regions the Goral (*Nemorhedus Goral*) should be
collected. The Terai, throughout its whole extent, is
the ground for numberless Elephant, Rhinoceros, Tiger,
Leopard, Panther, Cheetah or Hunting Leopard (*Felis
jubata*), Bear, Lynx, Hyæna, Sambur (*Rusa Aristotelis*),
Barasingha (*Rucervus Duvaucellii*), Muntjak (*C. vaginalis*), Four-horned Deer, Spotted Hog Deer (*Axis
maculata*), etc. The Himalayas furnish the most
superb examples of the Pheasant group, among which
is the grandest of all, the Monal or Impeyana ; a
splendid bird of this species, the *Lophophorus L'huysi*,
should be looked for on the northern slopes ; the
Horned, the Cheer, the Snow, Kaleege, Cocklass, etc.
Of other *Gallinæ*, there are many species of Partridges,
the Black Partridge, Chickor, etc., and Pea Fowl, as
well as an immense succession of perching-birds.
Among the *Pavoninæ*, or Pea Fowl, the *Polyplectron*,
often called the Argus Pheasant, which is peculiar to
Indo-Chinese countries and Malayana, may be found
here. But the true Argus (*Argus giganteus*) is to be
got only in the Malay Archipelago. Of *Raptores*, the
Golden Eagle (*A. chrysaëtos*), though rare in India, can

be collected on the Himalayas; and the *A. imperialis*
is also found. The great Condor, often measures more
than 13 feet from tip to tip of wings. The Houbara
Bustard (*Otis hubara*), the great Brown Vulture (*V.
Monachus*), the Tawny Vulture (*Gyps fulvus*), the
Bearded Vulture (*G. barbatus*), and others, as well as
many *Falconidæ*. At the north-eastern extremity of
India, in Assam, the country is mountainous, but
watered by the Brahmapootra and numberless tributary
streams. The forests are among the best grounds for
Elephant, and large herds are to be encountered there,
affording grand hunting. Not only in the forests, but
in the gigantic grass jungle which is peculiar to
Eastern Bengal, and extends to Assam, Tiger, Bear,
Buffalo, Hogs, Fox, and Jackal, are to be had in
plenty. Among the fine *Phasianidæ* to be got in
Assam, are the *Lophophorus Sclateri*, which has been
found on the Khasya hills, and the *Ceriornis Blythii*,
both rare. In Burmah are many tracts still absolutely
wild, almost untouched by man, and therein roam
Elephant, Tiger, Rhinoceros, Leopard, and other,
mostly smaller, *carnivora*: but no canine animals—
Jackals, Hyænas, Wolves, Foxes, etc.,—which are
curiously absent from this and the countries of tropical
Asia lying east of Bengal. The Long-Billed Brown
Vulture (*Gyps Indicus*) is very plentiful in Burmah;
but the Peacock (*Pavo cristatus*), so common throughout all India, is not found either in Burmah or Assam.

The Sunderbunds, or marshy deltas of the Ganges
below Calcutta, are a number of low islands covered
by a rank growth of wood and apparently irredeemable
jungle. The cover is full of great game, Tiger, many
Buffalo (*Bos Arnee*), bearing the greatest horns of the
Bos genus, Rhinoceros, Deer, Hogs, etc. Alligators

are numerous. Throughout Bengal most of the animals that abound in the Terai are to be collected, and the favourite grounds are to be easily found. The *Cervidæ* are plentiful, and of large size. In the Sunderbunds the Barasingha (*Rucervus Duvaucellii*) and Hog Deer (*Axis maculata*) are very numerous, and along the whole course of the Ganges; a great variety of animals can be got on the banks of this wonderful stream. In the west of India, to the north and east of the Gulf of Cutch, is the Runn of Cutch, alternately a sandy saline desert, with numerous shallow lakes, or a vast lake-like marsh. Upon the banks, and in the small islands of the Runn, the Onager, or Wild Ass, exists in great numbers; there are many Apes, Porcupines, and birds in vast flocks. The Lion is now almost confined to the extreme north-western districts. The Peninsula of Guzerat is the most notable ground; but isolated specimens have, even in late years, been collected where once the noble game was plentiful, farther to the east in the Central Indian districts. In the wastes and jungles of Hurreeanah, and on the wooded plains along the Bhardar and Sombermuttee rivers, to the borders of Cutch, Lion may be found. They were undoubtedly very numerous there sixty or seventy years ago. The Peninsula of Guzerat, or Kattywar, as the whole province is named, is covered with undulations of no great height, but of wonderful ruggedness, and made almost inaccessible by forest and jungle. In the ravines and caverns of these tracts great game is harboured, Lion, Tiger, Leopard, Cheetah, Wolf, Hyæna, Deer, Antelope, Hogs, etc. Nylgai (*Portax Tragocamelus*) roam in large herds over the northern parts. But the climate in these districts is often deadly to strangers, particularly after the autumnal

G

monsoon. The Flamingo, Argala, or Adjutant Bird, Sarus, or Gigantic Crane, and many aquatic birds can be collected.

Central India is a fine ground. The hilly country, or Satpurá Highlands, may be said to range across the Peninsula from near Calcutta to Bombay, lying between those provinces designated as Northern India, and those of the Deccan or Southern country. This truly central position is, as it were, a border land between Northern and Southern India. At one period the Lion, as well as the Elephant, was common in these districts; but now the first-named may, for all hunting purposes, be pronounced extinct there, although an isolated example was met in the Sagar district not many years ago. The Elephant is now found only in the extreme eastern part of this region. Buffalo (*Bos Arnee*), which once was plentiful, has retreated from all save the eastern parts. They are found in the Mandla highlands during the rains, but they retire thence to the jungles south and west when the tame cattle are brought up to graze. They roam, however, in the great Saul forests that clothe the vast plains lying below Amarkantak to the north and east. They are not found west of Jubbelpoor and Nagpoor in these districts. In these eastern forests wild Elephants may be encountered, and this is the westernmost range here of this mighty creature. The number of them has, however, greatly decreased since the Government drove these forests systematically in 1865–67. To the north and east of Laäfargarh extends the Elephant country, where also may be found Tiger, Panther, Sambur, Black Bear, and Red Lynx (*F. caraval*), Spotted Deer, Red Deer, etc. Generally in the more westerly parts of the district are to be found Tiger—

more numerous at Doní and Betul than in Mandla—
Cheetah or Hunting Leopard (*F. jubata*), Panther, Bear
(*Ursus labiatus*), Wolf, Jackal, Boars on the plains.
Barasingha (*Rucervus Duvaucellii*) may be met with in
the patches of Saul forest, but it is not very plentiful
there. Spotted Deer (*Axis maculata*) along the wooded
banks of streams, Barking Deer, Sasin, sometimes called
" Black Buck " (*Antilope Bezoartica*), but they have not
so fine antlers as those in North-Western India; Indian
Gazelle (*G. Bennettii*), Nylgai, Four-horned Antelope
(*Tetracerus quadricornis*), commonly called "jungle
sheep." Sambur is sure to be found in those localities
where the Gaur is to be encountered. This last-named
fine animal is one of the most characteristic and important, in a sporting sense, of Central India. He is
called by sportsmen the "Indian Bison," and he frequents
the hills, as the Buffalo loves the plains and swamps.
Gaur is numerous on the Mahadeo Hills, but he retires
before the advance of men and tame cattle—civilisa-
tion, in fact. Crocodiles (*Crocodilus biporcatus*), the
Magar of Upper India, can be shot in the Nerbudda
river. Tiger shooting proper commences in April,
but March is good. During October and November,
migratory wild fowl arrive and swarm on the rivers,
pools, and tanks. Several sorts of Teal, including
the Blue-winged Teal (*Querquedula crecca*), Duck,
Widgeon, etc., and Geese. Many Waders, including
the Coolen or Demoiselle Crane (*Anthropoides virgo*),
and the Sarus Crane (*Grus Antigone*). Gray Quail,
Painted Partridge, Jungle Cock, and Pea Fowl, afford
good sport of its kind. The grand Imperial Eagle
(rare in the South), the Florican Bustard, several
species of Vulture, Hawk, and Owl. Blue Jay, Red
Flycatcher, Mango Bird, Snake Bird, etc.

G 2

Southern India, viz., all that portion of the great peninsula below the 20th parallel, contains some of the finest grounds for big game, and, at the same time, some of the most convenient and healthy stations which the sportsman can make his head-quarters. On the eastern side, in the jungle on the deltas of the Mahanuddy, are many Tiger, Leopard, Buffalo, Crocodile, etc. Leopard is particularly plentiful in the forests of Cuttack, in Orissa. On the Deccan grounds, Tiger, Sloth-Bear (*Ursus labiatus*), Cheetah, Sambur, Nylgai, Spotted Deer, etc., and Hogs are numerous. Near the table-land of Mysore, on the wooded slopes of the valley through which the Moyar river runs, Elephant may be found, Tiger, Leopard, etc. On the Sheveroy Hills, in the Carnatic, Gaur may be got, as well as Tiger, Panther, Bear, Hyæna, Sambur, Spotted Deer (*Axis maculata*), Nylgai, and other Antelope. The Neilgherries, or Blue Mountains, furnish some of the most delightful stations in the world, and from Coimbatore, or Ootacamund (which last is the principal), some of the best hunting may be easily reached. The Wynaad jungle is a fine field. Therein may be met Elephant, Gaur, Tiger, Leopard, Cheetah, Panther, Hyæna, Wolf, Sambur, Spotted Deer (*Axis maculata*), Muntjak, and other *Cervidæ*; Neilgherry Ibex, a distinct species on the hills, afford fine sport; and the sportsman can get Partridge, Quail, Snipe, Woodcock, and Spur fowl in plenty. On the Annamullay Hills, and among the ravines at their base, great game is to be met, especially in the forest and jungle there, where Elephant can be had. All the immense forest south of the Neilgherries, extending over the Annamullay range along the Western Ghauts, is a very fine ground of glorious extent, and not yet over-hunted; therein are many Elephant, many Gaur, Tiger, and Panther ; Bears are most numerous. All these southern regions are indeed rich in *feræ naturæ*. Of *Aves*, the Spotted Eagle (*Aquila nævia*) should be collected, and the Tawny Eagle (*A. fulvescens*), especially in the Deccan. Malabar and the Neilgherries have several species of birds unknown in other parts of India, and the same, although in a much less degree, may be said of the Carnatic and Central Provinces.

CEYLON.—Elephant (*Elephas Sumatranus*) is the most important of the indigenous fauna, and exists in considerable numbers all over the island, excepting the populous parts. His favourite resort is the mountain tops ; there are, however, not so many now as formerly. The species is almost always comparatively tuskless. Buffalo abound in all parts of the island, but most in the solitudes of the Northern and Eastern provinces. Gaur is said still to exist in some districts, but if so it is very rare. Sambur, often called Ceylon Elk (*Rusa Aristotelis*), on the mountains; Spotted Deer (*Axis maculata*) and Muntjak (*C. vaginalis*), in the forests of the interior, are the principal *Cervidæ*. Of *Carnivora*, Bear (*Ursus labiatus*) are in the thick woods of the low, dry district on the northern and south-eastern coast ; Leopard (not Cheetah, as they are sometimes erroneously called), and a rare variety, quite black (*Felis melas*), can be got ; Mongoos (*Hephestes vitticollis*) is comparatively common ; Palm Cat (*Paradoxus typus*), Genette (*Viverra Indica*). Only one example of *Edentata*, the Pengolin (*Manis pentadactyla*), or Scaly Ant-eater, is found. There are four species of Wanderoo Monkeys : some which inhabit the lowland woods ; and others, the largest of which is the *Presbytes*

Ursinus, are met only on the mountain zone. The rare *Presbytes Thersites* may be sought for, and a white variety may sometimes be captured. *Cheiroptera* are very numerous; the most curious of them is the Rousette (*Pteropus Edwardsii*), commonly called the Flying Fox. The birds are numerous and interesting. There are remarkable Cetaceans in the sea, among which is the Dugong (*Halicore dugong*).

INDIAN OR MALAY ARCHIPELAGO.—This is a wondrous region, full of natural historical wealth, and probably, in many respects, less known to science than any other part of the world. The islands are of vast importance. Borneo is more than twice as large as all Great Britain. New Guinea is larger than Borneo. Sumatra is as large as our whole home empire; and there are numbers of other islands, like Java, as extensive as Ireland or Jamaica. The great islands, Sumatra, Borneo, and Java were probably at one period part of the Asiatic Continent, and in them the animals and other natural productions are, many of them, of the Asiatic forms—some of identical species. In like manner New Guinea was, doubtless, connected with Australia, and we find there the Australian forms, both of animal and vegetable. On the Malayan peninsula Elephant, Rhinoceros, and Tiger may be got, and a few of the last-named game on the island of Singapore. On the mainland some of the birds are of great beauty. The true Argus Pheasant (*Argus giganteus*) is in the thickest forests: it is very shy and wary, and runs among the trees so swiftly and quietly that it is very difficult to collect. It is generally snared. The beautiful Eastern Trogons may be obtained here, and should be looked for in the deepest woods; the Blue-Billed Gaper (*Cymbirhyncus*

macrorhyncus), the Green Gaper, Green Barbets
(*Megalœma versicolor*), and other rich birds should be
carefully preserved when captured. In the three
great islands already named, Sumatra, Borneo, and
Java, although the Asiatic forms prevail, there are
several distinctive races. The Mias,* or Orang-utan
(*Simia Satyrus*), is found only in Sumatra and Borneo.
Another species (*Simia Morio*), a little smaller, is only
found in the same islands; the large Siamang only
in Sumatra and Malacca. These great *Simiadæ* are
peculiar to these regions.

SUMATRA.—The Mias, or Orang-utan, the Siamang,
and *Simia Moria*, mostly in the low swampy forests.
Elephant (getting scarce), Rhinoceros (*R. Sumatrensis*,
two-horned) ; *R. Javanus* (one-horned) is said also
to be in the woods; Tapir (*T. Malayanus*) ; Tiger ;
the Black variety of Leopard (*F. melas*) ; Balu Leopard
(*L. Sumatrensis*) ; the rare Leopard (*F. macrocelis*),
sometimes called the Clouded Tiger, having markings
which partake of both characters ; the Flat-headed
Lynx (*F. Planiceps*) and Golden Tiger Cat (*F. aurata*)
are among the principal *Carnivora* ; the Black Ox of
Sumatra (*Bos Banting*), somewhat resembling the
Gaur. Of *Cervidæ*, the Banjoe, or Black Stag (*Cervus
Hippelaphus*), Samboe (*Rusa equinus*), and Spotted
Deer (*Axis maculata*) will be found; and Antelope
(*Capricornis Sumatrensis*) in the hill forests. Sun-
Bear (*U. Malayanus*) ; Squirrels are very abundant
and curious ; Argus, and some Ocellated Pheasants ;
Fire-backed Pheasants (*Euphocamus ignitus*) ; Bronze
Cock (*Gallus æneus*), and *Gallus giganteus*. There are

---

* Mr. Wallace records the following dimensions of a large old
Mias killed by him : height, 4 ft. 2 in.; arms, from tip to tip of
fingers, 7 ft. 9in. ; face, 13½ in. wide ; girth of body, 3 ft. 7½ in.

no Pea Fowl on this island, although it is nearest to the mainland. There are numerous smaller birds of great beauty and value.

BORNEO.—Mias and *Simia Morio* and the Long-nosed Monkey (*S. nasalis*), which last is found only on this island ; Elephant, Rhinoceros. Black Leopards can be often met with. Golden Tiger Cat, Flat-headed Lynx, Sun-Bear (*U. Malayanus*), and a second species (*U. Euryspilus*) ; the Sumatran Ox (*Bos Banting*) ; Samboe Deer (*Rusa equinus*), Spotted Deer (*Axis maculata*). Great Argus, and several pheasants.

JAVA.—Rhinoceros (*R. Javanus*), a distinct species. Tiger, Leopard (*L. Javanensis*), the Black variety (*F. melas*), and Bear (*U. Malayanus*), are the most important *Carnivora*. Banjoe, or Black Stag (*C. Hippelaphus*), Spotted Deer (*Axis maculata*), Muntjak (*C. vaginalis*), Wild Bull (*Bos Banting*). The birds and insects of Java are especially beautiful and various. The Peacock, not found in Sumatra or Borneo, reappears in Java; the species is distinct from the Indian. The Horn-bill (*Buceros lunatus*) ; *Gallus giganteus*; Jungle Cock (*G. Bankiva*) in plenty ; the rare Green Jungle Fowl (*G. furcatus*). The Yellow and Green Trogons (*Harpactes Reinwardti*) ; the superbly splendid little Flycatcher (*Pericrocotus miniatus*) ; Black and Crimson Oriole (*Analcipus sanguinolentus*) ; all these last-named are rare, and are among the most notable to be found only in this island, and probably only in the western parts of it. The Great Crowned Pigeon (*Lophyrus coronatus*) is easily to be met with in this and other islands, but abundantly in New Guinea; so is the remarkable *Geophilus Nicobaricus*.

NEW GUINEA AND NEIGHBOURING ISLANDS. — The forms of both animal and vegetable life on the islands in this division of the Archipelago are mostly of Australian character. But the principal glory of the region in a zoological sense is the possession of a purely distinctive race of *Aves*, the Birds of Paradise. These are all of great value and transcendent beauty, simply forming one of the most beautiful groups in the world. For a long period all that was reported of their habitat was very trifling, and intermixed with mere fable: though much more is known now, our information is comparatively scanty, and there is no region of the globe so little understood, and yet so calculated to well requite scientific exploration. Mr. A. R. Wallace who, a few years since, visited the islands for the purpose of investigating the *Paradisæ*, has recorded the best and latest information concerning their range and particular habitat, and the following is quoted from his words ("Proc. Zool. Soc.," 1863, p. 166): "The Aru islands contain *Paradisea apoda* and *P. regia*; and we have no positive knowledge of *P. apoda* being found anywhere else; Mysol has *P. papuana, P. regia,* and *P. magnifica*; Waigiou, *P. rubra* only. Salwatty, though so close to New Guinea, has no restricted *Paradisæ*, but possesses *P. regia, P. magnifica, Epimachus albus,* and *Sericulus aureus.* The island of Jobie, and the Mysory islands beyond it, certainly contain true *Paradisæ*, but what species beyond *P. papuana* is unknown. The coast districts of the northern part of New Guinea contain *P. papuana* and *P. regia* pretty generally distributed, while *P. magnifica, P. alba,* and *Sericulus aureus* are scarce and local. Lastly, the central mountains of the northern peninsula are alone inhabited by *Lophorina superba, Parotia sexsetacea, Astrapia nigra, Epimachus magnus,* and *Craspedophora magnifica*; and here also probably exist the unique *Diphyllodes Wilsoni* and *Paradigalla carunculata.*" The birds frequent the deepest woods and trackless wilds. The indescribably beautiful Hoopoe, Promerops (*Epimachus magnus*), can be got on the coasts of New Guinea, and should be carefully collected and preserved.

AUSTRALIA.—It is the head-quarters of the *Marsupiata* and of the Parrot tribe. The species of *Marsupiata* are distributed in greatest numbers in Western Australia and New South Wales; next in South Australia and Van Diemen's Land. In North Australia the species are neither so large nor so numerous. The Great Kangaroo (*Macropus giganteus*) is to be got in each division but the north; but another species of nearly equal size (*M. antilopinus*) is to be got there. The Great Rock Kangaroo, or Black Wallaroo (*M. robustus*), is found on the mountain ranges in the interior of New South Wales only. The Red Buck (*M. rufus*), also of the largest size, is found in many parts of the interior of Australia, but particularly New South Wales, where also another large species, the *M. Parryi*, abounds. Several species of Opossum and other smaller creatures can be collected. The very curious Duck-billed Platypus (*Ornithorhyncus paradoxus*) and the Porcupine Ant Eater (*Echidna Hystrix*) should be carefully preserved. The largest of the Australian *Carnivora* is the Tasmanian Wolf, or Zebra Opossum (*Thylacinus cynocephalus*), found now only in the highest mountainous parts of Van Diemen's Land. Of Birds the largest is the Emu (*Dromaius Nov. Holl.*), mostly in the south. The Lyre Bird (*Mœnura superba*) is found principally in the forests of the Blue Mountains, but also on the other mountain ranges generally of New South Wales. The curious Kivi-Kivi

(*Apteryx Australis*) on all the islands of New Zealand, but most at the southern end of the middle island. An almost infinite variety of Parrots and Pigeons can be collected, as well as many aquatic birds. The Laughing Kingfisher (*Dacelo gigantea*), the Satin Bower Bird (*Ptilonorhyncus holosericeus*), should be looked for, as also the Great Bustard (*Otis Australis*).

AFRICA.—This vast continent is the habitat of countless great quadrupeds, and altogether of a profusion of animal life that is perhaps unequalled on the globe. Vast regions of it are still unexplored, and there is ample verge for enterprise. The number of mammals is most remarkable, and of those peculiar to this continent the proportion is great. This is the true home of the Lion. The large Pachyderms are most numerous here; and the great Antelope tribe has its head-quarters in this division. Among the *Quadrumana* are the Gorilla and the Chimpanzee. In alluding, for the sake of convenience, to Northern, Southern, Eastern, or Western Africa, it should be borne in mind that, comparatively speaking, the great districts or natural divisions on the coasts are all that can be referred to with certainty; beyond all these, in the interior, lie fields for the hunter, where discovery of great natural facts may be pursued, while extraordinary sport is obtained.

In Southern Africa, and the countries contiguous to and above Cape Colony to either coast, may be found two varieties of Lion (*F. Leo*), one yellow and another brown, this last the fiercest. They are never met on the hills, but frequent the plains where there is rank grass, or where low bushes grow near water, and on the banks of rivers. Panther (*F. Pardus*), Leopard (*L. Serval*), the Lynx (*F. caracal*), usually

where Lions frequent, and the Booted Lynx (*F.
caligata*), Tiger Cat (*F. Serval*), Hyænas, the Striped
(*H. striata*) (but his true habitat is Northern and
Central Africa) and Spotted (*H. maculata*), and the
Brown (*H. rufa*). Elephant (*E. Africanus*), having
the finest tusks of any species. Rhinoceros, three
varieties may be encountered, mostly in the remoter
districts, viz., *R. Africanus*, two horns of unequal
length; *R. Keitloa*, two horns much longer and of
unequal length; *R. Simus*, one long and one short
horn. Hippopotamus, Buffalo (*Bubalus Caffer*), Giraffe
(*Camelopardalis Giraffa*), north of the Orange river;
Quagga (*Asinus Quagga*), and Pœtsi Zebra . (*A.
Burchellii*), on the plains, especially north of the
Orange river; the true Zebra (*A. Zebra*), on the
mountains. Antelopes are most numerous. On
the plains: Hartebeest (*A. Caama*), commonest;
Springbok (*A. Euchore*), in immense numbers; Pallah
(*Æpyceros melampus*), Grysbok (*Calotragus melanotis*),
Bleekbok (*Scopophorus Ourebi*), particularly in the
eastern parts; Gemsbok (*Oryx Gazella*), and the
remarkable White Oryx (*O. Leucoryx*), Blauwbok
(*Ægoceros leucophœus*), and other maned variety of
this species, the *A. barbata*; Waterbuck (*Kobus-
ellipsiprymnus*), 4 feet at shoulder; Steinbok (*Calotragus campestris*), where it is stony, and on hills;
Eland (*Orcus cauna*), largest of all, 5 feet at
shoulder; Rietbok (*Electrogus arundinaceus*), near
watercourses; Lechée (*A. Lechée*), on banks of the
Zouga. In the woods: Duykerbok (*Cephalopus
Grimmia*), Bushbok (*C. Burchellii*), north of Orange
river; Rhoodebok (*O. Natalensis*), and the beautiful
Koodoo (*Strepsiceros Kudu*), near rivers. Addax (*A.
nasomaculatus*), on sandy tracts of the interior; and

the remarkable Antelope, Korus Sing-Sing, should be sought for. Gnu (*Connochetes gnu*) and Brindled Gnu (*C. Gorgon*), on the plains north of Orange river; never south of Black river. Aard-Vark, or African Ant Eater (*Orycteropus Capensis*), and the Aard-Wolf (*Proteles Lalandii*), an animal interesting to zoologists from its place in nature's economy, can be got in the neighbourhood of Algoa Bay.

Many of the birds are very notable, among which may be particularised: Ostrich; Kori Bustard (*Otis Kori*), the largest of the genus, upwards of five feet high, very fine game, found especially in the countries on the banks of the Orange river; another, *Otis Denhami*, always where Gazelles are; and the African Bustard (*Otis cærulescens*). The gigantic Stork (*Ciconia Marabou*). Flamingo (*Phœnicopterus ruber*), multitudes in the neighbourhood of Walvisch Bay; and the small species (*P. parvus*) on the lakes; Demoiselle Crane (*Anthropoides virgo*), Secretary Bird (*Gypogeranus Serpentarius*), the superbly beautiful *Promerops erythrorhyncus*, and Golden Cuckoo; Bee-eater (*Merops apiaster*), Roller (*Coracius garrula*), in deep forests; Sun-birds, etc.

Western Africa yields the Gorilla (*Troglodytes Gorilla*), the Chimpanzee (*T. niger*), and two other great anthropoid Apes (*T. Aubryi*), and the rare one described by Du Chaillu, called by him *T. Koolo-Kamba*, as well as *T. calvus*, all of which are valuable. They are found in the most remote woods of the Gaboon district. The very handsome King Monkey, sometimes called Full-bottom, on account of its extraordinary wig-like hair (*Colobus polycomus*), and several other species of *Colobi* can be got near Sierra Leone. The Lion of Senegal is a distinct species, of yellower

colour than its congeners, but the mane is mostly
inferior. Panther (*F. Pardus*), Leopard, two species
(*F. Leopardus* and *F. neglecta*), Striped Hyæna (*H.
striata*), Lynx (*F. caracal* and *F. caligata*), Hippo-
potamus. Of Antelopes: the Mohr (*Gazella Mohr*),
Kevel (*G. rufifrons*), Red-crowned Bushbok (*Cephalopus
coronatus*), the White-backed (*C. sylvicultrix*), the Bay
(*C. badius*), the Black-striped (*C. Ogilbii*), the Black
(*C. niger*), the White Oryx (*Oryx Leucoryx*), Korrigum
(*Damalis Senegalensis*), and the Doria, or Gilded
Antelope (*Doria Zebra*), a perfect specimen of which
is rare in England, and should be sought for.

Of Birds in these countries: the Pheasant-like
Touracos, the beautiful *Corythaix Senegalensis*, *C.
erythrolophus*, a superb species, *Chizoeris variegata*,
and the magnificent *Musophaga violacea*, can be
found frequenting the highest trees about the Gold
Coast. The Spur-winged Plover (*Philomachus spinosus*)
should be sought for, and its habits, of which little is
known, recorded; Gigantic Stork (*Ciconia Marabou*),
Flamingo, Demoiselle Crane, Crowned Crane (*Balearica
pavonina*); Jabiru, a large wader, about the lakes and
marshes; Great Kingfisher (*Ispida gigantea*), Secretary
Bird, Roller, Sun-birds, etc.

In the Northern countries of Africa will be found:
Lion, a distinct variety, with deep yellowish-brown
coat and grand mane; Leopard, Lynx, *F. caracal*,
F. caligata, and *F. chaus*—the last-named most fre-
quently about marshes and bogs; Striped Hyæna
(*H. striata*), Wolf, Jackal; Gazelle (*G. Dorcas*), Addax
(*A. nasomaculatus*), plentifully; Bekker-el-Wash, or
Wild Ox, as the Arabs call him (*Alcephalus Bubalis*),
to the borders of Sahara; in Barbary, the Bush Goat,
or Barbary Deer (*Cervus Barbarus*), the only member

of the *Cervidæ* on this continent. Among the birds are—Flamingo, Demoiselle Crane, Crowned Crane, Roller, etc. Several Vultures, the Griffon (*V. fulvus*), *V. Kolbii, Neophron percnopterus,* and other of the Raptores.

Eastern Africa: Hippopotamus, in the Nile; Elephant, in Abyssinia, where also, on the hills, Mohr (*Gazella Sommeringii*), Andra (*G. ruficollis*), *G. Dorcas, G. Isabella,* Oryx (*O. Leucoryx*), and the remarkable Antelope (*Hippotragus Bakeri*) discovered (1868) by Sir Samuel Baker, are principal quadrupeds. The Ibis, Spur-winged Plover, many Storks, including *Ciconia Marabou.* Flamingo, in Egypt.

AMERICA.—The New World continent possesses several animals which afford grand sport for the hunter, but altogether the forms of animal life are not so highly developed as those of the ancient great divisions of the world. The birds, however, of Central and South America are more beautiful and resplendent with gorgeous plumage, as well as more various, than are those of any other countries. The ornithology of North America is also remarkable and valuable.

In North America, the Bison, or, as it is termed, Buffalo (*Bison Americanus*), ranges on the prairies of the North-west, but at present is seldom seen east of the Mississippi or south of the St. Lawrence, on this the most inhabited side of the continent. The districts of the Saskatchewan, and thence southward of the upper course of the Missouri, as low as Texas and Mexico, support immense herds. There are two varieties recognised by local hunters of the Red River districts, viz., that of the great plains, which generally avoids the woods, and that much scarcer, which frequents the woods; this last is only found north of the Saskatchewan and on the flanks of the Rocky Mountains. Great Slave Lake is the northern limit of these grand animals. Elk, or Moose (*Alces Malchis*), the largest of the *Cervidæ*, in the Canadian forests, Caribou (Reindeer), Wapiti (*Cervus Canadensis*), 4½ feet at shoulder, can be got in the woods skirting the Saskatchewan plains. A smaller variety in herds on the plains of California and upper parts of the Missouri; American Deer (*Cariacus Virginianus*), most numerous on the Pacific coasts; Mexican Deer(*C.Mexicanus*),White-tailed Deer (*C. leucurus*), Cariacou Deer (*C. nemoralis*), shores of Texas and Mexico; Black-tailed Deer (*C. Lewisii*), California; Mule Deer (*C. macrotis*), eastern slope Rocky Mountains. Grizzly Bear (*Ursus ferox*), Black Bear (*U. Americanus*), Polar Bear (*Thalarctos maritimus*), in the Northern Sea. Puma (*Felis concolor*), which takes the place of the Lion in the New World, can be met in the Southern States below New York. There are two varieties, and sometimes a black example is met with. Lynx (*F. Canadensis*), in the woody districts of Canada. Many of the smaller fur-bearing animals, among which is the large Otter (*Lutra Canadensis*), peculiar to the northern districts, and the Opossum (*Didelphys Virginiana*). The Water Fowl are innumerable and fine, of numberless species. Red Flamingo (*Phœnicopterus Chilensis*) in the warmer parts, but the colour is not so good as that of the European species. Among the *Raptores* will be found —Bald Buzzard (*Pandion Haliœtus*), the Sea Eagle (*H. leucocephalus*), the symbol of the United States, in every part of which it may be encountered, and the Golden Eagle. The Harpy Eagle (*Harpyia destructor*) must be sought in the thick forests of Mexico. The fine ivory-billed Woodpecker (*Picus principalis*) can be got in Mexico and some of the Southern States, but never north of Virginia. In Mexico and Guatemala may be collected the Trogons, perhaps the most superb of all birds. They are never found on open places or inhabited tracts, but are of solitary habits, frequenting the deepest woods. *Trogon resplendens,* the most splendid in colour and of finest form, should be sought for; *T. Mexicanus,* of exquisite and varied colouring, is in the north of Mexico; there are other species of almost equal beauty. The Wild Turkey (*Meleagris Gallopavo*) is plentiful in the North-Western States, and ranges to the Isthmus of Darien; another species of singular beauty, *M. ocellata,* may be got in Honduras. The Galeated Curassow (*Ourax Pauxi*) and the Crested Curassow (*Crax Alector*) may be collected in Mexico.

South America is not very rich in great game, but has overwhelming interest for the naturalist. Of *Carnivora,* the principal are Puma (*F. concolor*), as far south as Paraguay, in Chili, and generally throughout Brazil—the Gray variety is never got north of the Isthmus; Jaguar (*F. Onça*) is found generally about this half of the continent, but most numerously in Paraguay and the Brazils. There is a handsome black variety of this Cat to be met with frequently. Three species of Ocelot can be collected in Paraguay, and probably in Peru, viz., *F. pardalis,* the Gray (*F. armillata*), and the Painted (*Leopardus pictus*). The Chati (*F. mitus*), Pampas Cat (*F. Pajeros*), and several others of similar species, as far south as Patagonia. Otter (*Lutra Braziliensis*), is plentiful in the lakes and rivers of Paraguay. Llamas are in Columbia, Peru, Chili, on the Cordilleras of the Andes, but recently reduced in numbers; they are also in Paraguay, but

H

more rare. Tapir (*Tapirus Americanus*), all over South America, but never north of Darien. Of *Cervidæ*: The Guazupuco (*Blastocerus paludosus*) and Mazame (*B. campestris*), northern Patagonia; Tarush (*Furcifer antisiensis*), mountains of Bolivia; Guemul (*F. Huamel*), on eastern coast; Cariacou (*Cariacus nemoralis*), Guiana; the beautiful little Gauzu-viva (*Coassus nemorivagus*), Brazil; the Cuguacu-ete (*Coassus rufus*), large herds in the marshy woods; several species of Brocket in Brazil and Chili. The birds are wonderfully varied and beautiful. The American Ostrich (*Rhea Americana*) is numerous on the plains of La Plata, as is also the smaller species (*R. Darwinii*). Several fine *Raptores*: Condor of the Andes (*Sarcoramphus Gryphus*), one of the largest of the *Vulturidæ*, mostly in Peru and Chili; Caracara Eagle (*Polyborus Braziliensis*), on the coasts of Venezuela and Brazil, most abundant in the south and east of Brazil, and in Paraguay. Harpy Eagle, in Caracas, Guiana; Brazilian Eagle (*Morphnus Urubitinga*), *Asturina cinerea*, and numerous other *Falconidæ* in Guiana and Brazil. The naked-cheeked species are confined to the southern parts of the continent. Red Flamingo, Peru, Chili, coasts of Brazil, and Guiana; the great Stork-like Jabiru (*Mycteria Americana*) will be found generally on the marshes and round lakes; while about similar places in Brazil and Guiana those curious fine birds, the Horned Screamer (*Palamedea cornuta*) and the Chaja (*Chauna Chavaria*) may be met with, the last named in Paraguay, and La Plata as well; the Çariama (*Palamedea cristata*), a bird of retiring habits, frequents the mountain plains of Brazil, and is found in Paraguay, but is scarcer there. Of *Cracidæ*, the Crested Curassow (*Crax Alector*), and the Guan

(*Penelope cristata*), are in Brazil and Guiana; the *Ortalida Motmot*, a pheasant-like bird, and the Hoazin (*Opisthocamus cristatus*), and others, in Guiana; the Red-knobbed Curassow (*Crax Yarrellii*), in Peru. Ivory-billed Woodpecker (*Picus principalis*), in Brazil. The beautiful Cock of the Rock (*Rupicolla aurantia*), now becoming rare, in Guiana, especially about the river Oyapock; another of this species, the *R. Peruviana*, is in Peru. The Great Toucan (*Ramphastos Toco*), in the wooded districts of the river Plata and Guiana; others, *R. Cuvieri, Pteroglossus Humboldtii,* and the Black-banded Toucan (*P. pluricinctus*), about the banks of the Amazon. Several species of the exquisite *Piprina*, and other magnificent Chatterers, or Fruit-eaters, are in Brazil and Guiana. These last-named countries, with Peru and Chili, and the Tropical regions generally, are the home of the incomparable *Trochilidæ*, or Humming Birds, which are found mostly about the marshy deltas and the banks of the rivers. Thousands of gorgeous Macaws, and various species of *Psittacara*, or Parakeets, inhabit the warm districts of the Andes, the Brazils, and Guiana.

INDEX.

A.

Albatross, Trophies of, 45.
Alum Process, 18.
Anatomy, for Vital Shots, 4.
Antelope, 78, 81, 83, 84, 87, 92, 94.
Antlers, Packing of, 32.
Apparatus, 2, 27.
Arms, 2.
Arsenical Soap, 16.
Aurochs, 75.
Axis Deer, 79, 81, 85, 87, 88.

B.

Bacon Beetle, 19.
Barasingha, 79, 81, 83.
Barking Deer, 83.
Banjoe Stag, 87, 88.
Bear, 72, 75, 78, 80, 82, 85, 87, 88, 96.
Birds of Paradise, 89.
Birds: Collecting, 8, 9; decoys and dummies, 10; sexing, 14; preservative for skins, 16; protection of skins from insects, 17; skinning, 36–43; making the skin, 43; keeping in spirit, 46.
Bison priscus, 75.
Bison, 83, 95.
Black Buck, 83.
Blow-pipe, an implement for collecting, 8.
Buffalo: Vital Shots, 6; Hunting Fields, 80, 82, 84, 85, 92.
Burra-Sing, 78.
Burrell, 78.

C.

Camera, Photographic: part of sportsman's kit, 11.
Cape Buffalo: Vital Shots, 6.
Casting Fish, 67.
Cervidæ, Skinning, 29: Head Trophies, 31.
Cervidæ, American, 96, 98.
Cheetah, 79, 81, 83, 84.
Collecting: Arms and Apparatus, 2–12; importance of record and ticketing, 12–15; general observations, 13.
Curing by natives, 15.

D.

Decoys, 10.
Dermestes Ladratus, 19.
Dummies, 10.

E.

Elephant: Difference of Indian and African, 6; Vital Shots, 6; the Duke of Edinburgh's, 21; folding an elephant's skin, 21; skinning his foot, 30; Hunting Fields, 79, 80, 82, 84, 88, 92, 95.
Elk, 73, 96.

F.

Felidæ: Vital Shots, 5; skulls, 23; skinning and preparation, 29.
Fish: preservation of, 24; immersion in spirits, 25; packing, 25; skinning, 46; dressing with preservative, 47.

CHARLES DICKENS AND EVANS, CRYSTAL PALACE PRESS.

.